WHEN CONCORD WAS KING!

The origins and intriguing life of Ontario's native grape and wine industry

JIM WARREN - M.A.

When Concord Was King
Copyright © 2018 by Jim Warren

No part of this publication may be reproduced, distributed, or transmitted in any form or by any means, including photocopying, recording, or other electronic or mechanical methods, without the prior written permission of the author, except in the case of brief quotations embodied in critical reviews and certain other non-commercial uses permitted by copyright law.

Tellwell Talent
www.tellwell.ca

ISBN
978-1-77370-991-8 (Paperback)

TABLE OF CONTENTS

PART ONE 1

The roots of winemaking 1

    Preface: Embracing a journey rooted in mystery 1

    "Old World" winemaking: Ignorance is bliss! 5

    The New World: Home of the "Wild Child" 7

    The Southern Fox: North America's First Wine! 9

    "Northern Fox" grapes and native wine:
    A paradox in the making! 12

PART TWO 17

New vines to supplant the native grapes: 1600-1850 17

    1619: Vinifera Vines come to eastern North
    America: Encountering a hostile 'terroir' 17

    "A" is for Alexander! - The earliest North
    American hybrid grape! 21

    Coming of age in America: Remembering
    John Adlum and Nicholas Longworth 25

PART THREE   31

Introducing grapes to Upper Canada and Ontario: 1790-1880 31

    Fish, furs, forts, fighting, and…fermentation! 31

    Johann (John) Schiller: Father of the Ontario
    Wine Industry ... or not! 35

    The Isabella: One "Prince" of a grape! 42

    From brewing and distilling in early Niagara to … fermenting! . . . 45

    A plethora of new vines, both discovered 'by chance' and others
    'man-made': but not all grapes are created equal! 50

    The 1860s: A commercial grape and wine industry
    is "born" – but whose baby is it? 60

    Winemaking at Clair House, Cooksville:
    Prejudice, politics, and a prophecy! 66

    Clair House after de Courtenay: A struggle to survive 78

    Pelee Island: A pure, native wine industry on
    Canada's island in the sun 82

    North American hybrid vines: Friend or foe? 88

    The 1870s: More new wineries put down roots
    in the new province 94

PART FOUR   103

A century of development and denial: Ontario winemaking, 1880-1980 . . . 103

    Growing Pains: An industry in infancy confronts
    the winds of change 103

    Changing the game: Control, clean-up, consolidation,
    …and Chardonnay! 113

    Ontario Native wine in the 60s and 70s: transitioning from
    adolescence towards obsolescence 126

CONCLUSION　　　　　　　　　　　　　　　　143
Throwing the baby out with the bathwater, radically! 143

REFERENCE MATERIAL　　　　　　　　　　　153
When Concord Was King! 153

EARLY HYBRID GRAPES
IN EASTERN NORTH AMERICA　　　　　155
Early Ontario developed hybrids 161

ABOUT THE AUTHOR　　　　　　　　　　　163

PART ONE

The roots of winemaking

Preface: Embracing a journey rooted in mystery

> The 'fox' in Niagara Peninsula wines is troubling a British connoisseur. The critic, Cyril Ray, says all 15 Canadian wines he sampled had a characteristic North American back-taste called 'foxiness'. This taste was sweet and earthy and typical of the American vine. "So what?" replied a Niagara Peninsula wine expert.
>
> —The Hamilton Spectator, 1965.

My fascination with wine began in the early 1950s with a purple potion called Mogan David that my father served at Christmas for family and friends. I was young, and so was given only little to taste, but I loved the grapey flavour—sweet but pungent. I was, of course, totally unaware of wine's potential for providing more complex pleasures. For several years, this one elixir was my sole exposure to wine, a drink otherwise seldom seen in our house. From such an innocent beginning, who would have guessed that wine and its creation would become such a passion and obsession in my life? Or that wine would lead me on a journey from wine lover to amateur winemaker to professional winemaker, to consultant, and teacher?

Most recently, this journey has encouraged me to explore the beginnings of winemaking in 19th century Ontario, and to relate the story of our early grapes and the long-forgotten people who created a local wine industry long before the introduction of the vinifera grapes, grapes which made possible our modern, world-class grape and wine industry.

The story begins some 400 years ago in the early American colonies on a most mysterious note: the local wild grapes which grew so abundantly everywhere could only be made into wine that could best be described as unpalatable. In short order, the word "foxy" was used to describe the unique, unusual, and unappealing flavour and aroma associated with both the wild grapes and the resulting wine – another apparent mystery! One might well wonder why so many species of these wild grapes were indigenous only to America and nowhere else, or why Mother Nature did not include among them the one species used by people since the dawn of civilization for winemaking in the Old World, the grape: Vitis vinifera.

Equally as mysterious for people with no understanding of fungal diseases or pests like Phylloxera vastratix, was the inability of generations of Americans to grow vines imported from Europe as a substitute for the indigenous vines. Yet this exercise in frustration—attempting to grow the imported vines with no success when the same vines grew perfectly well in Europe—actually resulted in an accident of nature: the fortuitous creation of inter-specific hybrid vines, vines that were as welcome as they were mysterious.

For amidst all the disappointments, a chance discovery near Philadelphia in the 1740's of a new grape variety—the first of several hybrids to appear spontaneously over the next 100 years in different states—would alter the course of winemaking history with consequences for America and for the world that no one at the time could ever have predicted. These vines were able to survive and produce acceptable wine grapes, fostering a renewed passion for viticulture and stimulating an American wine industry. After the American Revolution, these grapes swiftly made their way north, brought along with the thousands of people who came to seek a new life in Upper Canada.

The actual origins of viticulture in Upper Canada are still cloaked in mystery; we simply do not know what grape varieties were first brought from the United States, nor who brought them or when, nor from where, nor even where they were first planted. It is not until grapes start being mentioned in early newspapers and in the promotions for various fairs and exhibitions that we can glean anything about the first individuals who grew grapes in Upper Canada, individuals who exhibited a passion for a fruit that, in the 1850s, was still considered something of a novelty.

From this point the historical roadmap offers a fascinating narrative of experimentation, entrepreneurial ambition, and innovation as the growing of grapes and the making of wine become important economic activities. This establishment of a new industry in Upper Canada coincided with the arrival of Confederation in 1867.

At this time, many of the grapes available had had a very short history. Several had been discovered only as recently as the 1840s and 1850s, grapes that were "tainted" with foxiness, making winemaking a challenge. Nevertheless, nothing deterred a small number of individuals such as Kilborn and Kitchen in Niagara and the Parker family in Cooksville, all of whom established well-sized vineyards and became our first winemakers despite whatever vinous prejudice existed. It is fair to ask their motivation. Did they sense some opportunity at this time in our history when there was still little consumer awareness or demand for wine in general, existing as it did in the overwhelming shadows of the omnipotent beer and alcohol businesses? Adding to this mystery was the negativity surrounding the pervasive use of alcohol in society and, although wine was considered less harmful than "demon" rum, it was nevertheless included in the increasingly vocal attacks by temperance advocates to ban all forms of alcohol in the province. Perhaps these first winemakers were bitten by that mysterious bug which has been infecting people for thousands of years, resulting in an obsession to make wine or perhaps, as true entrepreneurs, they simply hoped that locally-made wine might become a profitable business venture. In any case, to them we owe a debt of thanks for the first commercial wines that were made and sold successfully in Ontario.

Our native wine industry originated, in the words of the late Percy Rowe, "as a gentle craft," that is: family winemaking or cottage winemaking. With the arrival of several *labrusca* hybrids from the United States, and in particular the infamous Concord grape, family-scaled winemaking slowly blossomed into a tiny new industry towards the end of the 19th century. The industry mushroomed province-wide during Prohibition, again based largely on the use of King Concord. At this time, with the sales of other alcohol illegal, wineries proliferated rapidly in order to satisfy the hordes of thirsty drinkers.

The noxious wine produced during Prohibition led to a period of bureaucratic control. This in turn led, through the 1930's and the Second World War, to the consolidation of wineries and to the downsizing in consumption of Ontario wine. At that time a small number of visionaries—aware that the industry needed to change and improve the nature of its winemaking and that a reliance on the Concord grape could not achieve this—began to experiment with new hybrids and *vinifera* grapes that came primarily from France.

The next three decades following World War II saw increased plantings of many new vines. These proved successful and resulted in a revolutionized industry that usurped King Concord with many winemakers creating exciting new wines that would receive both public acceptance and, before long, world-wide acclaim. Rapidly forgotten in all of this were our native grapes and the original wine industry, which had served the province for 100 years, an industry cellared in mystery, surviving innumerable challenges, only to face a sad obsolescence.

In Canada there is a saying that we are long on geography but short on history, a truism, given we live in such a vast country with a traceable past of only 500 years. As a result, people often believe there is little history worth relating and have scant appreciation for the achievements of the previous generations. This is unfortunately a Canadian shortcoming, but it seems especially true of our winemaking history, whose beginnings are deemed to have no connection to our present industry. However, by shining some light on these origins, I hope to show that we do have history worth appreciating, and that we can certainly respect the successful efforts of many in challenging circumstances who provided their fellow citizens with the civilizing touch of local wine!

Jim Warren

"Old World" winemaking: Ignorance is bliss!

> It is also becoming increasingly clear ... that the world's first wine culture, comprising both viticulture and winemaking, emerged in this upland area by at least 7,000 B.C.
>
> —McGovern, *Uncorking the Past*, 2009

> Scientists have theorized for several years that our thirst for alcohol goes back much further, to the prehistoric days when early man tasted fermented fruit and enjoyed the taste ... and the buzz.
>
> —Carpenter, *Wine Spectator*, 2015

> Penicillin may cure human beings but it is wine that makes them happy.
>
> —Sir Alexander Fleming

Archaeological records dating back thousands of years—yes, long before the discovery of penicillin—prove that wine has been making people happy for a long, long time. Indeed, recent scientific research has established that some 10 million years ago the mutation of the **ADH4** gene in our primate ancestors allowed them to use fruit fermenting on the ground as a safe and enjoyable food source, thus beginning our exposure to the intoxicating effects of alcohol.

Fermentation is the intentional transformation of sweet liquids such as honey or grape juice through the addition of yeast into a beverage containing ethanol. It is impossible to say when this first occurred; however, recent amazing archeological discoveries have established that our species has been imbibing alcoholic beverages at least since early Neolithic times.

The Neolithic times are equated with the so-called dawn of civilization, a time when humanity was beginning to develop permanent settlements in China and the Near East. This step in human evolution led to farming and to the domestication of plants and animals; it also began the quest to create alcoholic beverages. These beverages were made from an array of fruits, honey, saps, and cereal grains and flavoured with the ingenious use of additives such as tree resins, herbs, and spices. How and when this process was discovered must now be left to our imagination.

From the beginning, these manifestations of beer and wine were considered to be gifts from the gods, a glorious mystery that people lacking scientific understanding could only accept and appreciate. Successful fermentation would have been the result of instinct, inherited experience, and experimentation. It would have been almost an art form, given the challenging issues involved in fermentation. Indeed, it would have been an endless struggle to achieve stability and age-ability, and to avoid spoilage; yet the resulting beers and wines quickly became popular and highly valued as an alternative to water as well as revered for their association to divinity. Obviously, they were also pleasurable given their mystical, intoxicating alcoholic impact.

At some point, the superior potential of grapes for making wine would have become apparent. Although not as readily available as cereal grains, grapes are naturally blessed with very appropriate sugar and acid levels and would have produced relatively good results despite their makers ignorance of fermentation science. As well, grapes are laden with natural yeasts capable of surviving and generating a "healthy" alcohol level.

Grapes are limited to a short harvest period; thus grape wine would have been more expensive to produce than beer, and would have yielded smaller quantities. However, as production increased and prices fell, wine became available to all classes and not just to the elite. And the discovery of pottery (circa 6000 B.C.) would only have facilitated wine production, making possible storage and transportation and wine's establishment as a necessity of everyday life.

Today all grapes are considered part of one large botanical family bearing the name *Vitis*, the Latin word for vine. Within this family are many different species, yet all wine grapes from European vineyards belong to just a single species now identified as *vinifera*, again a Latin term meaning wine producing. This one species, perhaps originating in Asia Minor as the wild *Vitis vinifera sylvestris*, spread rapidly west from the Mediterranean to Europe where it became the cultivated grapevine of ancient and modern agriculture. This is the grapevine associated with Dionysus, Bacchus, and

Noah, the grapevine that eventually developed into the 5,000 or so varieties known to us now.

It is difficult to imagine making wine with no knowledge of chemistry, no electricity, and no sophisticated equipment. As well, there were few known additives to control bacteria or create stability and few ways to ensure a reliable harvest. Yet by the time the first European explorers and fishermen were sailing west to the Americas, wine was a part of everyday life, a source of good health and good cheer, with its effects well known and appreciated. And although most wine must have been of dubious quality—thin and coarse, and often unstable or acetic—it quickly became an essential part of the daily diet, and with that came a growing demand. Certainly by the 1500's there was a sophisticated trade in wine. Even amidst ongoing European wars, wine made its way to the New World. Spain had full control of South America by this time and was shipping thousands of casks of European wine to Mexico to lubricate its thirsty armies. Wine was highly desired in Spanish society where the statement: "The rich want good wine; the poor want lots of wine" would have been perfectly understandable to all classes.

No wonder that the first Europeans to arrive in what is now known as North America were so delighted to find grapes growing in abundance everywhere. Indeed, almost as soon as these first Europeans landed they turned their hand to making wine from local grapes, attempting what was now so natural, if sometimes naturally awful, in spite of their ignorance of the fascinating life of yeasts and bacteria!

The New World: Home of the "Wild Child"

> The history of the vine in America begins, symbolically at least, in the fogs that shroud the medieval Norsemen's explorations.
>
> —Pinney, *A History of Wine in America*, 1989
>
> America is one vast Vineland.
>
> —Adams, *The Wines of America*, 1978

Numerous references in the records of first explorers to North America document sightings of wild grapes growing in profusion in what became known as the New World. Of course, these first explorers would not have realized then that North America is endowed with over 20 different native species that grow wild between 50 degrees latitude north in Canada and 25 degrees latitude south in Florida, a wider range than anywhere else on earth. Nor did these first explorers seem concerned that the grapes looked and tasted differently from the grapes in their home countries. It appears that they were impressed with what they saw; and they were pleased!

Interesting evidence suggests that the sightings began over a thousand years ago when Leif Eriksson and his wily crew landed in what is today known as Newfoundland. In *The Greenlanders' Saga,* a narrative of Leif's voyage to the west, Leif relates the story of a man named Tyrkir the German who wandered away from the others for some time, returning with the news that he had found grapevines and grapes. To this day there is controversy over the location of Tyrkir's discovery. Some even question whether what he found were actually grapes and believe that Leif meant blueberries or some other fruit. However, in the story Tyrkir himself says that he was born where vines and grapes are no rarity, a testament to the credibility of the tale—he knew what he saw—and Leif himself was inspired to name the land "after the good things they had found there," the good things being grapevines, hence the name, Vinland!

If they were grapes, we can only guess what wild species they might have been, given they were able to thrive at such high latitudes. However, we can say for certain that the grapes did not belong to *Vitis vinifera* since this species is not indigenous to this continent. Although the wild vines are true grapes, in North America they had developed quite differently from the grapes of the Old World, which all belong to *Vitis vinifera,* and which historically had been grown primarily for winemaking.

There is no evidence that the native peoples here ever used grapes to satisfy their thirst, even though grapes grew prolifically everywhere, having adapted to the varying soil and climatic conditions. New World grapes generally lacked the sugar content of the *Vitis vinifera*—a sugar content that is a pre-requisite for generating healthy alcohol levels and ensuring stable wines—and were acidic in the extreme, making for tart, unappealing wines that were often cursed by an unusual musk-like aroma and flavour, wines that were simply not up to the standards of wine made from the traditional *Vitis vinifera*.

Of considerable significance later in our wine history will be that no *Vitis vinifera* is native to North America where, in spite of the variety of grapes available, all would prove to be decidedly "wild!"

The Southern Fox: North America's First Wine!

> We found such plenty (of grapes), as well there as in all places else, both on the sand and on the greene soile on the hils, as in the plaines, as well on every little shrubbe, as also climbing towards the tops of high Cedars, that I thinke in all the world the like abundance is not to be found.
>
> —Hakluyt, *The Principal Navigations, Voyages, Traffiques, and Discoveries of the English Nation*, 1589
>
> ... and so began the long chapter of hopes and failures written in the English colonies down to the Revolution.
>
> —Pinney, *A History of Wine in America*, 1989

From the late 1400's on, many would note the abundance of grapes in the New World. In 1524, Giovanni da Verrazano—a Florentine explorer employed by King Francis I of France—sailed up the eastern coast from what is now South Carolina to Newfoundland, thus earning credit as the first European to see New York harbor; he also provided one of the earliest existing accounts of the Native Americans. In a letter to the King he reported: "many vines growing naturally there," and called the country "New France." It is interesting to speculate that if the French had actually settled along this coast rather than the English—who did not have any great experience in growing grapes or making wine—if colonial winemaking would have started on a more successful note than it did. Or, given the nature of the grapes, perhaps the French, unlike the English, might not have bothered with winemaking at all.

Soon, the French and New France were left to encroach further north where other interests would take precedence over winemaking. On his second trip down the St. Lawrence in 1535-6, Jacques Cartier noted grapes growing in profusion on what he named appropriately *Ile de Bacchus*, today called Isle d'Orléans, which is near modern Quebec City. But Cartier had little time for winemaking and later on others, including Samuel de Champlain, would continue to show far greater interest in fish, whales, furs, and in finding a passage to the Orient than in agriculture.

Almost three decades later a group of 200 French Huguenots were sent out by a French Admiral named Gaspard de Coligny to establish a colony at the mouth of the St. John's River in northern Florida. Near modern day Jacksonville they built Fort Caroline, the first permanent European settlement in the present day U.S.A.. Here they found wild grapes and, according to the report of a pirate named Captain John Hawkins, quickly produced twenty hogsheads of wine. Unfortunately, they were unable to produce food for themselves and were near starvation when Hawkins helped them out. A year later, in 1565, the Spanish destroyed the fort and, being no friends to Protestants, committed the first mass religious slaughter in North American history. No one doubts that grapes were available to the colony at that time, but there are many who do not believe that the French were able to make any wine. And there is another story concerning how, after the slaughter, the Spaniards built their own settlement on nearby Santa Elena Island—modern day Parris Island in South Carolina—where, in 1568, they planted a vineyard. It is possible they made the first local wine there; however, since it is impossible to verify both tales, we are left to make an educated guess about what kind of grapes produced the first North American native wine.

Of all the species that would eventually be named and classified in North America, one in particular, *Vitus rotundifolia* (round-leaf), proved a winner. It was perfectly adapted to the challenging, semi-tropical climate of the southeastern states, and flourished there on vines that grew like trees, spread for hundreds of square feet, and produced a prodigious amount of grapes on just a single vine. These were the grapes that Sir Walter Raleigh's men found growing on the islands near the Virginia coast in 1584 (in what is known today as North Carolina) and that they described as a carpet of grapes growing to the water's edge. The grapes are still there today, including the famous "Mother Vine," a huge, old *rotundifolian* growing on Roanoke Island where Raleigh attempted to found a colony in 1587.

Like other wild species, these grapes are distinctive. Unlike most other wild grapes, they produce palatable, commercial wine and have for a very long time under the more common name of *Muscadines*. This species possesses an extra pair of chromosomes—20 as compared to 19 for *Vitis vinifera* and other North American grapes. This variation gives them a thicker skin that protects them from the sun, heat, humidity, diseases, and insects. The grapes are large, round, and luscious, ripening individually in loose clusters containing few grapes (unlike most 'bunch' grapes), and have an exotic, strong, muscat-like or musky flavour and scent.

The history of winemaking from *rotundifolia* is fascinating and well-delineated in Thomas Pinney's book. The grape produces a most interesting variety of colours, and it and its wine is often referred to simply as *Scuppernong*, a word derived from a native term. Although it has never played a part in Ontario winemaking, has never been grown here successfully, and does not readily hybridize with *Vitis vinifera*, *Scuppernong* or *rotundifolia* represents a defining moment in the development of the American wine industry. In the hands of an entrepreneur named Paul Garrett, *rotundifolia* produced, for a time, the most popular wine in the United States. This wine was sold under the name *Virginia Dare* (the name of the first child born of English parents in America) and was advertised with the slogan: "There is more of this brand of wine used in the United States than of all other brands of bottled wines combined!"

In recent years *Muscadines* have grown in popularity and today hybridizers continue to create new varieties, christening them with names like Tarheel, Magnolia, Noble, Carlos, and Delicious. These *Muscadine*s range in colour from black, to red, to freckled, to pearl, and to the more traditional bronze. In several southern States they are made into very popular, if sweeter wines. Because of their sweetness, however, they are not much used for the elegant, dry, table wines so much in demand now, and their unique flavour, which earned them the unfortunate distinction as the southern fox grape, is not widely appreciated.

But to the first colonists, such grapes truly represented a great hope, given that wine, along with silk and olive oil, made up the trilogy of most desired commodities at that time. These commodities would inspire the colonization of America, until the new land revealed the truth.

"Northern Fox" grapes and native wine: A paradox in the making!

> I have been informed by such as have bin in Virginia, that there grow infinite number of wilde Vines there, and of several sorts; some climbe up to the top of trees in the woods, and they bring forth great quantities of small blacke Grapes...another sort of Grapes there is, that runne upon the ground, almost as big as a Damson, very sweet, and maketh deepe red Wine, which they call a Fox-Grape. A third sort there is, which is a white Grape, but that is but rare...
>
> —John Bonoeil, *His Majesties Gracious Letter to the Earle of South Hampton commanding the present setting up of Silke works, and planting of Vines in Virginia,*1622

> A second kind of grape is produced throughout the whole country, in the swamps and sides of hills. These also grow upon small vines and in small bunches and are of a rank taste when ripe, resembling the smell of a fox, from whence they are called fox grapes.
>
> —Robert Beverley, 1722

> There is another property of this grape which alone is sufficient to prove it to be the *Vitis vulpina*, that is, the strong rancid smell of its ripe fruit, very like the effluvia arising from the body of the fox, which gave rise to the specific name of this vine."
>
> —William Bartram, *Domestic Encyclopaedia*, 1803-1804.

In 1607 three ships with 144 passengers and crew (no women!) crossed the Atlantic from England and by May finally reached land in the New World.

They named the spot where they decided to build a fort Jamestown after King James, establishing the first permanent British colony in America (Virginia). In spite of terribly difficult conditions, mainly with the resident native peoples and their surroundings, the colonists began to prepare for their new life motivated by visions of fabulous wealth generated by the wonderful bounty of the New World. This bounty included silk, olive oil, possibly gold, and certainly wine. They believed this wine could easily be made from the profusion of wild grapes of various sizes and colours which grew everywhere: along sandy beaches and in swamps, up trees in the woods, and along riverbanks.

Indeed, early records indicate that some of these colonists quickly turned their attention to winemaking, no doubt harvesting the sweet, round muscadine grapes and others, which they assumed would make wine just like Old World grapes. The famous John Smith, one of the original settlers of Jamestown, tells us that by 1608 they had made nearly twenty gallons of wine and there are comments that indicate a doctor Boone and others had made wine in twenty-gallon lots by 1610. This was accompanied by exciting talk about taming or cultivating the native vines in vineyards. By the following year a law promised a death sentence for anyone who "robs any vineyards or gathers up the grapes."

This initial excitement contrasted with the disappointment that followed over the quality of the wine itself, summarized most often by the word "sour." Some of the wine that was sent to England was accompanied with the comment that "it was rather a scandal than a credit to us," and most of the wines appear to have been simply terrible. The British colonists, not known for their oenological expertise, would have had a difficult time working with wild grapes that were (and still are) naturally high in acidity and typically low in sugar. The resulting wine would have been thin, sharp, low in alcohol, and quick to spoil. On top of that, the wines must have been very different from Old World wines in aroma and flavor, what with their distinctive, unusual, and unflattering musky character.

Disappointed with the vinous results, the colonists came up with a word to describe this pervasive character: "foxy," a term that was hardly scientific but one that obviously reminded them of something familiar. In short order, and many years before the notion of species was fully developed, this descriptor was applied to a number of grapes including the *Muscadines* that came to be called the Southern Fox. Other grapes that grew further north were labeled the Northern Fox. In time these grapes would be classified into species *Vitis rotundifolia* and *Vitis labrusca*, yet the intriguing descriptor 'foxy' sets them apart as unique and remains as a description that haunts our wild grapes to this day. Later—after the discovery and/or development of new American hybrids, which were based in part on the *labrusca* species—the same term foxy would be associated with the aromas and flavours of the wines that these hybrids produced; thus this unflattering muskiness became unique to eastern North American wine.

Over the years a number of theories, from simple to fanciful, were advanced to provide a plausible explanation for what the early colonists really meant by the word "foxy." Originally it was believed that the word "fox" simply meant "wild," or that the grapes attracted foxes or that foxes liked to eat them. Some thought that the descriptor was associated with the Old English verb "to fox," meaning to intoxicate. Another suggestion was that fox was a distortion of the French word *faux*, meaning false, as if the wild grapes were not really grapes at all! In the end it became clear that the smell of the grapes and of the resulting wine was similar to the smell of the spray of the European fox. However, it would take until the twentieth century to corroborate this when some intriguing science led to a credible solution to the mystery. (see appendix)

How unfortunate for us that Mother Nature chose the wrong species to grow wild in eastern North America, denying us the pleasures of *vinifera* grapes from the beginning of colonization. If the colonists had arrived to discover different varieties of *Vitis vinifera* growing everywhere, one can only imagine how different the course of grape growing and winemaking here would have been; later, if there had been no foxy hybrids discovered or created from the wild vines, how different, as well, the course of grape history in the last two centuries would have been, not only in North American but also world-wide, as we shall see.

Those who had hoped that local wine, made from the native grapes, would become the daily beverage of moderation were definitely disappointed and obligated to turn to imported Madeira or to hard cider, rum, or whiskey for consolation. Leon Adams has made the comment that if the wine had been good, not only would the history of winemaking in North Eastern America have been of a different nature but also America might never have needed saving from the evils of beer and booze, nor witnessed the devastation Prohibition created later on. It is interesting to speculate whether tobacco would have become established as the colony's primary crop if vineyards could have produced wonderful colonial wine, wine that would have served as a lucrative source of income for the English government. Unfortunately, it did not take long for the colonists to understand that the native grapes made inferior wine that was only palatable if it was sweetened or 'brandied' and that the resulting beverage was hardly one of moderation.

In the years that followed, people in every colony would attempt to make native wines from the indigenous grapes, but with predictable results, carving in stone the amazing paradox of wild American grapes—vigorous, ubiquitous and abundant but yielding wine of little value. If America was ever to advance in viticulture it would certainly not be with the so-called fox grapes!

PART TWO

New vines to supplant the native grapes: 1600-1850

1619: Vinifera Vines come to eastern North America: Encountering a hostile 'terroir'

> We have seen that all of our European forefathers brought with them a love of the vine, or more correctly, a love of wine, and that throughout the 200 years in which America was being colonized many experiments were made in all parts of the eastern United States to grow varieties of *Vitis vinifera*.
>
> —Hedrick, *The Grapes of New York*, 1908

> One must also emphasize the fact that the early settlers of whatever nationality had every sort of natural disadvantage to contend with in seeking to adapt the European vine to a new scene…Thus the very fact that America had native vines…was the cause of the European vine's failure there.
>
> —Pinney, *A History of Wine in America*, 2007

Faced with a royal request to fulfill expectations of lucrative colonial winemaking, yet realizing that the wild vines made unsuitable wine, the men of the Virginia Company seized upon an idea that early governor Lord Delaware had suggested in 1616. Since the New World appeared to be a Garden of Eden for grapevines, they decided to bring over vines from Europe and transplant them to American soil using experienced growers recruited in France to work their *magique*.

According to company records, eight *vignerons* from Languedoc were to be sent to the colony with "vineplants of the best sort" in 1619, and the Governor himself, Sir George Yeardley, arrived that same year with vines, the earliest record of importing *Vitis vinifera* vines to this part of America. A law was passed requiring every householder to yearly plant and maintain ten vines in the manner that the French *vignerons* instructed. In 1622, King James I commanded his Master of Silkworms, John Bonoeil, to provide a manual on growing grapes and making wine so that "every man may presently have reasonable good wine in Virginia to drink."

Probably to everyone's surprise and dismay, these first efforts were unsuccessful; the vines simply failed to survive. A number of excuses were advanced to account for the failures, including poor vine management and disagreements between the French *vignerons* and the English colonists. In the end, it was decided to keep trying with further legislative encouragement and other inducements, along with additional plantings and renewed help from Europe. Again and again the repeated efforts bore little fruit, and it became more and more obvious that *vinifera* grapes would not flourish in Virginia.

Certainly the colonials did not realize the enormity of the challenge they had taken on in trying to grow the European vines in such an unfamiliar *terroir*, and one that was proving inevitably fatal to these vines. The climate itself, with extremes of weather including punishing cold winters and humid summers, is often even today a nightmare for growers. The native grapes had adapted to the climate, as well as built up levels of resistance to a variety of diseases and pests that were unknown in the Old World. Thus there were no remedies for powdery and downy mildew, nor for the black rot, which is so destructive to *vinifera* vines and fruit. And, of course, no one had any idea of the existence of pests like *Phylloxera vastatrix*, the vine-killing microscopic mite that would devastate European *vinifera* vineyards later in the 19th century. In short, the combination of a harsh climate, native pests, fungal infections and poor soils, not to mention the lack of scientific knowledge and general viticultural expertise, would mean that attempts to grow *vinifera* here were an exercise in futility.

Similar efforts in other colonies with imported vines over the next century would meet the same fate no matter the location, or the numerous varieties of grapes tried, or the skills and passion of the people involved, and no matter how much financial support came from England or colonial assemblies. European grapes would be imported again and again, only to produce little fruit but considerable frustration and disappointment. In fact, it would not be until the early 20th century when innovations such as rootstocks, pesticides, and other technological advances would give *Vitis vinifera* vines a chance to grow successfully in eastern North America, and even then at considerable risk! The surprising thing is that, in spite of consistent failures, so many people would continue to try, with both with wild grapes and imported vines, to fulfill the dream of making acceptable local wine. Yet it was not until the time of the Revolution that anyone was able to develop any kind of successful winemaking industry.

The history of the many attempts at viticulture in 17th and 18th century America is non-the-less fascinating, full of tales of passion and woe, optimism and disappointment, of lives spent attempting the impossible in conditions we can't imagine, of individuals who left their mark on their own times, only to become forgotten. In his detailed study of this period, *A History of Wine in America*, Thomas Pinney remarks that with the brilliant success of winemaking in America today it is only fitting "that the many obscure and forgotten people and their work lying behind that success should be brought out into the light." And we must agree.

In northern North America—that is French Canada or the future Upper and Lower Canada— there was nothing to compare to the American struggle to coax grapes from reluctant *vinifera* vines. No such efforts happened here, given there was neither the time nor the place for viticulture. For over 250 years until 1759, the French had shown little interest in agriculture, preferring to build forts down to Niagara and further west and south in an attempt to hem in the American colonies, and to direct most of their remaining energy at fur trading. Any wine of consequence was imported from Europe. Perhaps the French did not wish to provide any competition in New France for their already well-established wineries back home! But there were few colonists outside Quebec and, given the hostile environment, growing grapes and making wine were simply not important considerations, unlike the efforts being made further south.

There are a number of references to grapes and making wine that typically involve missionaries who needed wine to celebrate mass, and who often must have found themselves lacking. A Recollect named Nicolas Viel, who spent some time in Huronia, commented as early as 1623 that "when the wine which we had brought from Quebec in a little barrel of twelve quarts failed, we made some of wild grapes which was very good." It is seldom that you encounter any winemaker who believes his wine was anything but good, but in this case the wine filled an obvious need and was thus *bound* to be good! And there is the comment of the Jesuit Paul le Jeune (Huronia, 1636) that verifies the quality: "In some places there are many wild vines loaded with grapes; some have made wine out of them through curiosity; I tasted it and it seemed to me very good!" Another Jesuit named Father Jacques Bruyas commented some thirty years later that "there are also vines which bear tolerably good grapes, from which our fathers formerly made wine for the mass. I believe that, if they were pruned two years in succession, the grapes would be as good as those of France." The latter comment is reminiscent of those made in Jamestown where the wines were also not so highly praised. Obviously these Frenchmen were simply better winemakers than their counterparts in Virginia!

Shortly afterwards we find the Sulpician missionaries Francis Dolier de Casson and Rene Brehant de Galinee spending the winter of 1669 near present-day Port Dover on Lake Erie and again making wine from local grapes. This time the quality had apparently improved even further, given that the wine was described "as good as vin de Grave"! A Recollect missionary named Louis Hennepin—well known for his comments on Niagara Falls and his travels with La Salle—also makes several references to making wine in the 1670's from wild grapes. However, it would be more than a century before any grape growing or winemaking, such as had already developed in several American states, would become a reality in this area.

For grapes and for people this was a challenging era, with both trying to survive in a hostile environment. Efforts to grow *vinifera* grapes—whether in Virginia, Massachusetts, Maine, Maryland, Alabama, Georgia, New

Hampshire, South Carolina, New York, Rhode Island, North Carolina, New Jersey, or Pennsylvania—did meet with occasional short-term success, but all had proved fruitless in the end. Yet by 1750 the colonies had over a million people and a new nation was rapidly evolving in spite of an ongoing series of confrontations, bloody battles, and wars involving everyone: natives, the French, the English, and the Americans. Peace would come only after significant changes in the landscape. With the first Treaty of Paris in 1763, the French finally lost North America; with the second Treaty of Paris twenty years later and the end of the Revolution, the British lost their American colonies. Countless numbers of people lost their lives. in 1791, borders were established between the United States and what would become Upper and Lower Canada, setting the stage for a more civilized way of life.

But if good wine were to be a part of civilized life, it would still have to be imported from across the Atlantic ... until an unexpected outcome of all the viticultural work in the colonies, brought a most welcome surprise to American oenophiles.

"A" is for Alexander! - The earliest North American hybrid grape!

> There hath been no Burgundy made in Maryland since my arrival except 2 or 3 hogsheads which Colonel Tasker made in 1759; this was much admired by all that tasted it in the months of February and March following, but in a week or two afterwards it lost both its colour and flavour so that no person would touch it and the ensuing winter being a severe one destroyed almost all the vines.
>
> —Gov. Horatio Sharpe, Maryland

By the late 1600's, those intent on growing grapes in America were beginning to believe that viticulture would have to be based on American varieties, yet they continued to experiment with "foreign stems and sets." Such were the thoughts of William Penn (1644-1718), who had brought French vines with him to Pennsylvania in 1682 intending "to try both and hope the consequence will be as good wine as any European countries of the same latitude do yield." Penn had a Huguenot named Andrew Doz plant the vines in a vineyard along the banks of the Schuylkill River outside Philadelphia. Once again the *vinifera* vines did not prosper; however, this planting set in motion an accident of nature that, a few years after Penn's death, would help initiate a new era in the history of American viticulture.

For those struggling to grow grapes in America, the discovery of a new grapevine which actually made palatable wine had proven elusive. Thus, when the moment actually arrived, it was completely unexpected. Some time around 1740, James Alexander, the gardener for Thomas Penn, went walking in the woods in the neighbourhood of Springettsbury near the Schuylkill River. Imagine his excitement upon finding a vine growing on an outcrop overlooking the river near the vineyard that had been planted by William Penn. The grapes, he noticed, appeared different from the usual wild grapes. Being a talented nurseryman—and fortuitous for grape history—he decided to propagate the vine. Soon he was making decent wine. In 1756, a certain Colonel Benjamin Tasker of Maryland planted a two-acre vineyard on his sister's estate of Belair about 12 miles from Annapolis. He used cuttings of what was now called the "Alexander" grape, although it is not known how the vines made their way from Philadelphia to Maryland. In 1759 Tasker succeeded in making a wine that was good enough to be served to the governor of Pennsylvania in Philadelphia. Unfortunately Colonel Tasker died in 1760, and his vineyard failed; however, the Alexander grape, sometimes called Tasker's grape, would survive and change once and for all the prospects for making wine in eastern North America.

The Alexander grape is now considered to be the first American hybrid grape, an interspecific hybrid, originating spontaneously from a wild vine, probably *Vitis labrusca*, and an unknown *Vitis vinifera* vine from the plantings of William Penn, the father of Thomas. It is likely that one of those imported vines had pollinated the native vine, an accident of nature that is called a "chance hybrid." There are references to it being black/dark red and also musky or foxy (hence an alternate name: the Schuylkill Muscadel), as well as noticeably sweeter, and with compact bunches of medium-sized oval berries that ripened at the end of October. As a hybrid, it would display characteristics of both parents; in this case, the ability to survive American conditions like a native grape as well as the capability of producing a better wine like a *vinifera*. It was said to make a good wine of the claret type.

Thomas Jefferson even commented that wine made from the Alexander grape was "worthy of the best vineyards of France."

The years between the discovery of this grape and the Revolution of 1775 were marked by an optimism that winemaking could somehow succeed in spite of the difficulties in growing European vines. This indomitable American spirit was epitomized by no less a man than Ben Franklin who, as early as 1743, provided instructions on making wine in his *Poor Richard's Almanack*. Over the next twenty-five years he continued to foster the expectation that decent wine could be made in America. Indeed, samples of wine made from local grapes produced by several individuals were proudly exhibited at the American Philosophical Society in Philadelphia in 1768.

Ten years earlier the London Society for the Encouragement of the Arts, Manufactures, and Commerce had offered a prize to any colonist who could produce five tuns (barrels) of red or white wine of acceptable quality. They later developed a second prize for anyone who established a vineyard with at least five hundred vines. The winner, Edward Antill of New Jersey, was truly a remarkable man with a passion and zeal for grape growing that knew no bounds. He experimented with different vines, including local vines, and provided both cuttings and instructions to other enthusiasts. In 1769 he wrote the first American treatise on viticulture: "An Essay on the Cultivation of the Vine, and the Making of Wine, suited to the Different Climates in North America." Unfortunately, he died a year after its publication.

Another prizewinner, one William Alexander, had a larger vineyard of 2100 vines in New Jersey. He shared Antill's passion and fears. Both men commented on the ridicule anyone starting a vineyard would face due to the common belief that grape growing was a complete waste of time, effort, and money; and yet they continued to urge their fellows to do just that. Sadly, after the death of both Alexander and Antill, and with the arrival of the Revolution, both their vineyards fell into decay. It would be up to the Alexander grape to make a change for the better, a change that would endure.

Shortly after the Revolution in 1786, a Frenchman named Pierre Legaux bought an estate of 206 acres at Springmill about fourteen miles from Philadelphia and began planting three hundred vines, the start of an ambitious endeavour to form a private corporation and—with some impressive backers at that time like Aaron Burr and Alexander Hamilton—to establish a vineyard, winery, and nursery entitled The Pennsylvania Vine Company. Over the next 30 years the company and Legaux were often in trouble, both financially and with Mother Nature, losing many vines and often having to start over again. Along the way he obtained some Alexander vines that he named Constantia and introduced, perhaps fraudulently, as the Cape Grape from the Cape of Good Hope. In fact he sold large quantities of it at premium prices as a foreign variety—a much easier sell than a native vine!

In 1796 he had a visitor looking to buy vines, a man named Jean Jacques Dufour from Switzerland who was planning to move his family to America to grow grapes and make wine. After researching the best location for this, Dufour acquired 10,000 vines from Legaux for his commune in Kentucky and, in 1801, he moved his family there. Unfortunately, most of the 35 varieties he planted soon died, with the exception of the Alexander, and so the Dufours headed back to Switzerland. Some of the family moved on to Indiana and planted the Alexander grape. In Indiana, the Alexander grape was also planted successfully by a religious order of Harmonists, who would make some 3200 gallons of Alexander wine in 1812.

The ultimate failure of the Legaux operation reflected again an almost 200-year-old pattern with growing *vinifera* in eastern North America—initial success followed by disappointment. It did not matter whether the project was grandiose and well funded, or whether it was the effort of an organized company or a religious community like the French Huguenots and German Protestants with experience in viticulture, or whether it was an individual labour of love. Although repeated hundreds of times, the conclusion was always the same: the baffling reality that *vinifera* grapes could not survive in America. Legaux's nursery, however, was a step up as well as historically important since it supplied so many wine growers with the Alexander grape, the first grape to offer any real hope of successful winemaking in America.

Around this same time, President Jefferson—who had been trying himself to grow grapes, bringing vines and even soil from Chateau D'Yquem to help—finally found success with ten vines of Alexander. In 1809 he commented: "It will be well to push the culture of the Alexander grape without losing time and efforts in the search of foreign vines which it will take centuries to adapt to our soil and climate." Jefferson was a better president than prophet, for as we know now it would take just over a century more until the very 'foreign vines' he mentions would indeed be adapted to eastern North America, and finally initiating our commercial *vinifera* winemaking here.

As for the Alexander itself—in spite of the Presidential support and significant developments in Pennsylvania up to 1830 with several vineyards around York and Lancaster growing variations on the name Alexander—the grape would lose popularity with the discovery of new chance hybrids that were capable of producing even better wine and better at stimulating a widespread interest in viticulture. But the Alexander had been the first, and its discovery was truly a defining moment in the history of American grapes and wine and opened the door to a surprising future.

Today, as far as anyone knows, there is not a single vine of Alexander growing anywhere.

Coming of age in America: Remembering John Adlum and Nicholas Longworth

> Very good in its way is the Verzenay, or the Sillery soft and creamy; but Catawba wine has a taste more divine, more dulcet, delicious, and dreamy.
>
> —Henry Wadsworth Longfellow: "Ode to Catawba Wine"

By 1800, the world had become a much more interesting place in which to live. Over the two previous centuries commodities like chocolate, coffee, tea, and various versions of alcohol (brandy, rum, gin) had arrived on the scene in Europe. The wine world itself had witnessed several significant developments. The most important—the invention of the microscope in the 1600's—led to new discoveries in wine chemistry and microbiology. By 1785, the French chemist Lavoisier was able to establish how the sugar molecule split into gas and alcohol. The understanding of fermentation would come later on in the 19th century following the work of Pasteur. However, courtesy of Jean-Antoine Chaptal, steps had been made to manage and improve fermentation by applications of sulphur and by the additions of sugar to increase alcohol levels. Thus was born the term "chaptalization," initiating the mania for using French words\ to describe virtually every aspect of winemaking!

A revolution in the manufacturing of glass bottles in England had already led to advances in glass composition and in the proliferation of bottle shapes and uses. The manufacture of glass changed from the art of unique, free-blown creations to the science of molded, high-quality, inexpensive wine bottles that were mass-produced in bottle factories. Along the way, other improvements and inventions occurred, such as the use of cork stoppers for wine bottles and the corkscrew—first patented by an English clergyman in 1795—as means to remove them. The world was being prepared for wine cellars where wine bottles could actually be laid down for the maturing of wine in properly corked bottles, wine connoisseurs to appreciate such wines, and wine snobs to talk about them in boring detail!

In Eastern North America over these two centuries, life had been focused on domesticating a new world, as such there had been little success in developing a grape and wine industry that could take advantage of the European discoveries. With the Alexander grape, however, at last there was a chance for North Americans to participate in the ever-improving winemaking scene in Europe. In fact, after the Alexander's arrival, it is possible that one or two other discoveries had taken place but, except for the odd reference to their names, they have now disappeared in the mists of time. One that appeared just before the Revolution was called the Bland or Bland's Madeira, named for Colonel Theodorick Bland, and was reported growing in vineyards in New Jersey and Pennsylvania, and was possibly disseminated by Pierre Legaux.

And then came John!

A military man, a soldier in the American Revolution, a judge, and a surveyor, Pennsylvania-born John Adlum (1759-1836) possessed a life-long interest in agricultural science. By 1798 he had retired to a farm in Maryland where he pursued his interest in grapes. Subsequently he moved to Georgetown, Maryland to a 200-acre estate he named "The Vineyard," and there in 1814 he started his grape experiments. Adlum had already encountered problems with insects and diseases on *vinifera* vines he planted, and this experience led him to plant native vines, one of which was the Alexander. He confided to Jefferson that Americans did not yet seem willing to accept local wine, and that they rejected it when they were told it was native wine, even though they had enjoyed it up until the revelation!

In 1819 he found a grapevine growing beside an inn operated by a Mrs. Scholl in Clarksburg, Maryland. He offered to prune the vine for her, retaining some cuttings for himself. In 1821, he made wine from the Constantia grape (as the Alexander grape was also known), but it turned to vinegar. In 1822 he announced in periodical *The American Farmer* that he had made wine from a new grape that he called Tokay, and that the wine was better than any wine yet made from a native grape. A visiting German priest had said the grapes looked exactly like the Hungarian Tokay grape, hence the name. Adlum sent samples to Thomas Jefferson and others. Jefferson thanked him for the wine, which he found to be "truly fine wine of high flavor." Adlum reproduced the letter in the front of a book on winegrowing that he published in 1823. This book, *A Memoir on the Cultivation of the Vine in America and the Best Mode of Making Wine,* was the first post-colonial book on winegrowing in the United States.

In the second edition of this memoir, published in 1828, Adlum changed the name of the Tokay grape to Catawba and, in so doing so, changed the course of grape growing and winemaking in the Northeast. He had traced the actual origin of the grape to somewhere on the banks of the Catawba River in North Carolina where, around 1802, it was discovered by chance by a man named Murray. In 1807 a General Davy had obtained cuttings and planted them on his Rocky Mount property on the Catawba River. Sometime between then and 1816, when he became a U.S. Senator, he took cuttings to the Washington area and one of them ended up at Mrs. Scholl's inn where Adlum found it. The grape is an interspecific hybrid, probably *Vitis labrusca* and an unknown *vinifera*. It shows decent fruit quality, but has the *vinifera* susceptibility to various diseases. Light purple-red in colour, it yields a white juice with some foxy character and an appealing, spicy aroma.

Apparently Adlum's winemaking was not generally highly esteemed by others, although the grape itself quickly developed a strong following. John liked to chaptalize his juice so much that it remained artificially sweet, and he recommended fermentation at very high temperatures at which the yeast probably worked themselves to death! Yet John wrote that his work represented "a desire to be useful to my countrymen" and for a few years after 1825 he was the recognized authority on the subject of wine and vines in America. As a result of his efforts, there was such a growth of interest in winegrowing in areas as far as Maine, Florida, Ohio, Kentucky, New York, and Tennessee that John finally had to notify the public that the demand for cuttings was growing beyond his supply.

Indeed, on John's watch, the fire of American viticulture, which had been smoldering for two centuries, finally caught fire. Writing to Nicholas Longworth John noted: "In introducing this grape [Catawba] to public notice, I have done my country a greater service than I should have done had I paid the national debt." It is doubtful that American winemaking would have developed so rapidly at this time if the Catawba grape had not been propagated and sold by Adlum. In his in-depth *A History of Wine in America,* Thomas Pinney remarks: "All over the country waves were felt and echoes heard from the stir that Adlum had made. From South Carolina to New York, farmers, nurserymen, and journalists paid a new attention to the grape." Constantine Rafinesque, a contemporary of Adlum's who had worked in his vineyard to acquire experience, reported in 1825 that there were no more than 60 vineyards in the country totaling not more than 600 acres, but by 1830 there were 200 vineyards, up to 40 acres in size, and a total of 5,000 acres. Much of this growth was thanks to the presence of the Catawba grape. For his efforts, many believe that John Adlum should be considered the father of American viticulture.

After John's death in 1836 his name fell into obscurity; his home was demolished; and the farm eventually became a park. However, the significance of his work lived on.

One man who had received Catawba cuttings from Adlum in 1825 was Nicholas Longworth of Cincinnati, Ohio. Longworth (1782-1863) was a lawyer and real estate tycoon with a keen interest in horticulture, grapes, and strawberries. He had made wine in 1813 from the Alexander grape, which he fermented 'white' in an attempt to improve the quality of the wine that otherwise required the addition of sugar and brandy, resulting in something he called "a tolerable imitation of Madeira." But he quickly saw the potential of Catawba to make wine that even a temperance devotee could enjoy, and by 1850 he had expanded his plantings to 40 acres.

This work inspired several others to follow suit, so that by 1859, 2,000 acres of Catawba had been planted in the Cincinnati area and Longworth had offered a reward of $500 to anyone who could find a better native variety than the Catawba. There were no takers! Longworth believed he had found the secret to mitigating the musky taste of the grape—separating the skins from the juice before fermentation to produce a white or blush-coloured wine. His first success came when the expanding German immigrant population in the Ohio River valley wanted a decent wine. You might say he had the only game in town. In short order and, aided by French winemakers, he made the first champagne in the United States, a sparkling Catawba. Soon he was producing 100,000 bottles a year and his white Catawba was selling throughout the country. Cincinnati was producing over half a million gallons a year by the end of the 1850s when disaster struck – black rot and powdery mildew – decimating the vineyards and ending Cincinnati's reign as the wine center of the U.S.

Nicholas Longworth made Adlum's Catawba into the "wonder" grape of the time and became famous in so doing. His sparkling champagne sold to New York hotels for $12 per case, a very high price in those days. In 1858 a writer for the English *Illustrated News* declared "the Sparkling Catawba, of the pure, unadulterated juice of the odoriferous Catawba grape, transcends the Champagne of France." And there is, of course, the famous "Ode to Catawba Wine" by Longfellow. When Longworth died in 1863, two years after the outbreak of the American Civil War, most of his vines were dead and Longworth's properties were abandoned by his heirs. And so yet another pioneer of the grape and wine industry seemed headed for oblivion. The labour shortages caused by the Civil War, the seemingly incurable grape diseases, and the threat of Prohibition resulted in the closure of Longworth's bottling plant. However, the Catawba grape would survive in other locations, going on to become part of a glorious future in American winemaking history, and producing wines that people in the United States still enjoy today.

Within a few years Catawba grapes would cross Lake Erie to Pelee Island to play a significant role in our own local winemaking history and, along with other new North American hybrids that were contemporaries of the Catawba, would make their way into Upper Canada in the early decades of the 19th century.

PART THREE

Introducing grapes to Upper Canada and Ontario: 1790-1880

Fish, furs, forts, fighting, and...fermentation!

> To Europeans of the late eighteenth century, the challenge of early British North America seemed clear. It was to encompass the unknown, exploit the resources, develop commerce, and settle the wilderness. It was met, magnificently.
>
> —Wynn, *The Illustrated History of Canada*

> Grape growing and winemaking were hardly priorities in those early years, though there must have been settlers who made wine from wild grapes on an informal basis.
>
> —Hughes, *The Early History of Grapes and Wine in Niagara*

Before 1800, life in what would eventually become Canada could be described as one never-ending battle involving man against nature, as well as native people fighting to maintain their traditional way of life, and Europeans of various origins continuing European hostilities while attempting to exert their control over a new land. The founders of New

France, in attempting to establish their fur trading empire in North America with a loose-knit collection of forts from Quebec through the Great Lakes and down the Mississippi, maintained a long and deadly rivalry with the British who had established their own foothold with the Thirteen Colonies along the coast.

After the treaty of 1763, when Great Britain ultimately prevailed, settlers began to populate the British Province of Quebec. The settlers included people from Britain anxious to begin a new future and, after the American Revolution in 1775, British soldiers, Anglo-Americans, and others loyal to the Crown who were forced to flee from the United States. Our country nearing the end of the eighteenth century was already developing a multi-cultural character that included members of the First Nations. Still, although it was beginning to change under British Imperial authority and control, life at this point was still difficult, austere, and violent.

The Constitutional Act of 1791 quickened the pace of change from the French pre-occupation with furs and forts to a colony that, even in its infancy, would be concerned with developing civilized settlements. The British Province of Quebec was split into two provinces: Lower Canada—the seat of former French government—and Upper Canada, where John Graves Simcoe, with experience in the American Revolutionary War, was appointed Lieutenant-Governor. He and his wife Elizabeth reached Quebec in the fall of 1791 and made their way to Niagara-on-the-Lake in early 1792. They were determined to make his province a model of British government. Settlement had started here shortly before the end of the Revolution to grow food for Fort Niagara on the east side of the river. The first census showed less than 100 people. By the time of Simcoe's arrival, the British had purchased the entire Niagara Peninsula from the Mississauga First Nations and had surveyed for townships and for individual 100 acre lots to be arranged in concessions. The peninsula itself remained sparsely populated but, as the villages of Newark and Queenston slowly developed, farmers began to grow crops, especially wheat. Soon, however, Simcoe realized that Newark (the name he gave to Niagara-on-the-Lake) made an unsuitable capital for the new province given that it was vulnerable to attack from the Americans, and so he moved the capital to Toronto in 1793, renaming the settlement "York" after George III's second son, Frederick, Duke of York.

Introducing grapes to Upper Canada and Ontario: 1790-1880

To help encourage settlement and trade throughout the province, and to aid in defending Upper Canada, Simcoe began the construction of Yonge Street (named after the Minister of War, Sir George Yonge) along the north-south fur trade route from Lake Ontario. He also began construction of Dundas Street (named for his good friend Colonial Secretary Henry Dundas) along the east-west stretch between the head of the lake (Dundas) and the river La Tranche (now the Thames). Work on Dundas Street was started on September 23, 1793 with 100 soldiers laboring under the leadership of Captain Samuel Smith, a fact recorded in Elizabeth Simcoe's diaries. These diaries— which contained many details of the Simcoes' life along with drawings she made—are one of the earliest and certainly most valuable documents of early Canadian history. Referring to the road building, she makes what is the first mention of any grape winemaking in the area at that time. The same day that the road was started she tells us that she gathered wild grapes that were "pleasant but not sweet." On the 27th of October she goes on to say: "Captain Smith is returned from cutting the road named Dundas. It is opened for 20 miles. They met with quantities of wild grapes and put some of the juice in barrels to make vinegar and Captain Smith told me it turned out a very tolerable wine." It would appear that even with the ongoing threat of an invasion from the United States, soon to be a reality, there was time for a little fermenting by the military!

In 1796 John Simcoe, in ill health, returned to England where he died some ten years later at the age of 54, without ever returning to Upper Canada. He had served with enthusiasm and efficiency, leaving a significant record of achievement, a legacy that lives on to this day across Ontario.

Other than the soldiers' activity, there is no indication that viticulture or grape winemaking was of concern to anyone here before the end of the century. Upper Canada was still very much a wilderness, unlike the American colonies, which had already seen 200 years of efforts with both native and 'imported' vines. It is unlikely that many of the Loyalists moving north brought grapevines with them, as they did with plants and seeds, for there were hardly any such vines yet available. The Revolution was barely ended and there was still talk of war in the air; thus, any opportunity to obtain vines and bring them to Upper Canada would have been extremely rare.

Yet surprisingly, as early as late 1792, the first Agricultural Society in Upper Canada was established in Newark with the encouragement of Simcoe himself and, by 1794, it had arranged for the importation of fruit trees from Long Island. Here was located a rather well-known nursery named the Linnaean Botanic Garden. It was operated by the Prince family and grew and sold numerous horticultural specialties. The catalogue put out by William Robert Prince in 1830 listed 513 varieties of grapes for sale, including both American and *vinifera* species. It is very probable that the nursery—like the Pierre Legaux operation in Pennsylvania—was selling vines at this time, but whether any vines accompanied the fruit trees is simply not known.

As a result of very careful research, Brock University professor Alun Hughes has discovered some very interesting information concerning the grape growing that occurred after the turn of the century. He mentions a William Claus, Deputy Superintendent of Indian Affairs for Upper Canada, who maintained an elaborate garden at his Niagara home and who wrote in his gardening notebook on April 22, 1806 this comment: "Sowed next the gate to the left 3 rows of grape seed and a row of Orange Seed." We probably will never know what the seeds were, nor their source, nor how successful the planting was, but it does show that someone had an interest in growing grapes at this time.

Much more interesting is the reference to Thomas Merritt's claim for the loss of grapevines during the War of 1813. The Merritt farm was located east of Twelve Mile Creek in what is now St. Catharine's where he claimed for damages done to his buildings, fences and crops, including fruit trees and grapevines. Unfortunately, he does not mention the vines by name, but it would appear that these were cultivated vines, not native. Nor does he indicate how long the vines had been planted or in what amount. And there is another war claim by a Robert Kerr of Niagara Township who suffered losses of four vineyards. We can only speculate at what he meant by "vineyard" or what kind of grapes were planted.

These references, as limited as they are, hint at the beginning of grape growing in Upper Canada with grapes undoubtedly sourced from the United States beginning to make their way across the border prior to the hostilities of 1812-1814. Yet, we still cannot say with any confidence what our very 'first' grape might have been, nor its specific provenance, nor who planted it and when, although the choice of grapes at that time was very limited.

Johann (John) Schiller: Father of the Ontario Wine Industry ... or not!

> His vineyard eventually became one of magnitude and flourished with plump Clinton grapes of fine flavour.
>
> – Kathleen A. *Hicks Dixie: Orchards to Industry*
>
> By 1811 Schiller, who had previous winemaking experience in the Rhine, was fermenting grapes he had presumably grown from cuttings of wild vines and early American hybrids furnished by settlers from Pennsylvania.
>
> —Aspler, *Vintage Canada,* 1983

The beginnings of grape growing in Niagara early in the 19th century—as suggested by the references available, sketchy in their own right—have been overshadowed by another version of such beginnings. This competing story itself has enjoyed popularity for some 80 years now, and it has been told, retold, and embellished by writers attempting to capture this history. If it is true, it pinpoints the origins of the wine industry as beginning some 200 years ago, although this time frame, the location of the events, and its very nature, are shaded with disbelief. Despite this, the story of Johann Schiller has been accepted at face value by many who probably did not look into the historical reality behind it. Only recently has one individual, Professor Alun Hughes of Brock University, come forward to suggest that there is really no actual proof of Schiller's supposed achievements, and, in fact, there *are* numerous errors in the story. In reference to Schiller being considered the so-called father of commercial winemaking, he concludes: "it turns out that Schiller may have done little to merit any such distinction."

With so much interest being shown in this period in our local history, especially concerning the War of 1812-1814, it is appropriate to try to set the record straight, if such a thing were possible!

Beginning in the 1780's, the British Crown entered into a series of transactions with various First Nations peoples involving land ownership. These transactions would encompass much of what would soon be called Upper Canada. It required land to be provided in grants to some 10,000 British sympathizers, loyal to the Crown, who had poured into the province of Quebec, and who had left behind their property, livelihoods, friends and families in their escape from the Thirteen Colonies. Such grants would also encourage settlements and discourage, hopefully, attempts by the United States to continue aggression northward.

In 1787, the Crown arranged for the purchase of some 250,000 acres of land that included the area where Toronto is today from the Mississauga—an Ojibway tribe—for cash, various articles like kettles and mirrors, and 96 gallons of rum. The treaty, often referred to as the "Toronto Purchase," proved controversial from the beginning for several reasons and was revised on August 1, 1805, to correct a dispute over the western boundary of the territory at the Etobicoke Creek.

But there was also a need to deal with the Mississauga on the land to the west of York where in 1798, Dundas Street, after Simcoe's departure, had been opened from York to Burlington Bay by the Honourable Peter Russell. It now ran directly through lands populated by the Mississaugas of the New Credit First Nation (the Mississauga Tract). In a second meeting on August 2, 1805, the Crown purchased over 70,000 additional acres to the west of York under Treaty Thirteen A, the "First Mississauga Purchase," obtaining 26 miles of Lake Ontario shoreline and everything up to five miles inland, while leaving the Mississauga with the Credit River Indian Reserve, one mile of land on either side of the Credit, along with native fishing rights to a number of creeks that emptied into Lake Ontario. The "deal" made it possible for legitimate settlement and development to occur almost immediately. Three new townships were named by the Honourable Alex Grant, administrator of the First Executive and Legislature Council of Upper Canada, including Toronto Township immediately to the west of York.

To encourage settlement here, the government had Samuel Wilmot (1774-1856)—who had taken over his father-in-law's surveying commission in 1804—draw a map of the new Toronto Township with the recently opened Dundas Street as a centre line. Using chain measuring, Samuel and his crew completed the survey in six months, laying out two concessions to the North and three to the South down to the lake, and then divided the land into 200 acre (81 ha) lots, to be granted to incoming United Empire Loyalists and other pioneers. The lots were impressive in size, each one being 20 chains or 1320 feet wide and 50 chains or 3300 feet deep.

The first lots on both the North and South side of Dundas Street, which was straightened in 1806 to accommodate the grants, were designated the same year. They numbered from east to west starting with 1 North Dundas Street and 1 South Dundas Street in Concession 1. Many were occupied through 1807. The first census held here in 1807-1808 showed seven families. By 1809 there were 185 residents, including 60 children, living in what the new settlers called The Home District. To receive ownership (King's patent) of the property, the settlers had to first clear at least five acres and build a log cabin 16 x 20 feet in size, then clear the roadway in front of the site, and then provide a certificate signed by witnesses that this had been done. In this way a community gradually developed, originally called Harrisville. In the 1830s it was renamed, Cooksville.

Two anonymous Toronto newspaper articles on winemaking in the Cooksville area—the first in the *Evening Telegram* on September 10th, 1929 and the second in *The Globe* on April 22, 1934, well over a century later—suggest that the origins of our present-day Ontario grape and wine industry were literally carved out of the wilderness. The information in these two articles, like a good rumour, has spread and evolved into the amazing Schiller story that we have today.

Johann Schiller, born in the Rhineland, was one of the original grantees along Dundas Street, having obtained land for his military service in the American Revolution as a corporal in the British Regulars, 29th Regiment of Foot. He had spent some time serving along the St. Lawrence River where it is possible he met his wife, Mary Angelique. Here, after the war, he obtained a grant of 400 acres of land near Montreal in 1789. A few years later, being unable to develop his grant, he left Lower Canada and moved to Niagara Township in Lincoln County where he worked as a shoemaker. He then petitioned for land to replace his original grant but was obligated to wait several years before being approved. John, as he was named on the Order of Council document, moved to Toronto Township in 1807 with his wife and their seven children—John, William, Michael, Lucinda, Eliza,

Charles, and David—after receiving two grants of land on July 22, 1806 for Lot 9 and for Lot 17, both on North Dundas Street, Concession 1. The grants were signed by Deputy Surveyor Thomas Ridout, soon to become the Surveyor General.

John first completed his settlement duties on Lot 9 taking his certificate and witnesses to York on May 31, 1810. One year later he carried out his obligations for Lot 17, moving there in 1811. He then sold Lot 9 to James McNabb, a good friend, on April 17, 1812, just two months before the United States would unilaterally declare war on Britain. Lot 17 stood about a mile to the east of the Credit River. All of these facts can be supported by documentation and indicate that Schiller was a very able man and pioneer, who was doing his best to provide a good life for his family. Additional references to him and his life on his property are scarce, likewise after his death on October 12, 1816. In fact, no records of any kind mention or indicate any interest in or activity associated with grape growing or winemaking on his part until the first newspaper article in 1929!

Considering this complete lack of documentation, it is only fair to ask: how did any writer come to involve a pioneer named John Schiller in any story of grape growing and winemaking in Toronto Township in the early 1800s? Did someone have access to information that we no longer know about? Was this simply a mistake? The result of some confusion of information? Or was it a complete fabrication for whatever reason? One thing is certain. The story has been taken at face value by virtually everyone who has encountered it ever since.

The story tells how one day John was out hunting near the Credit River when he discovered wild grapes growing in profusion and took cuttings home, which he then cultivated on his property. At that time, he even made a little wine since he would have been (supposedly) familiar with grapes from his home in the Rhineland. In short order, and in spite of the difficulties of making wine with wild grapes in a challenging environment, he is said to have sold wine to his neighbours. While this activity would have been interesting in itself, it hardly qualifies as anything commercial in nature and does not merit the accolades it has received. In truth, it is the embellishments that have been added over time that have given the story mythic proportions, thus making the entire episode rather suspect.

It has been suggested, for example, that John actually received vines from Pennsylvania, but there is no mention of any vines by name. At this point in time, certainly the Alexander grape was available as Pierre Legaux was operating his nursery there, selling a variety of vines including the Alexander and several *vinifera*, but there is no evidence of any of these coming into John's hands. More difficult to believe is the notion that Schiller actually sold vines of his own creation to the United States. No less a respected authority than Angus Adams, former Director of the Research Station in Vineland, wrote in the *Canadian Collector* in 1984 that "Schiller experimented with grafting and hybridizing to obtain grape selections compatible with the harsh climate ... he developed and promoted a variety he called Clinton ... many of his vines were exported to the U.S." We are left to wonder where Angus discovered this information—that has become accepted parts of the Schiller story—as there is simply no documentation to support or verify these statements. Moreover, could John have possibly achieved all of this in the few years he had left before his death in 1816?

And what are we to make of his developing the Clinton grape? A "fact" referred to by Kathleen Hicks, a writer from Mississauga. Schiller might have been familiar with the word 'Clinton' from the township of the same name in Niagara (named by Governor Simcoe), but otherwise how do we explain the choice of this particular name? The grape itself, a dark blue-black hybrid of *Vitis labrusca* and *Vitis riparia*, dates in reality to the 1830s and to the town of Clinton, New York State (or to a Governor of New York State named Clinton), several years after Schiller's death. A while later the grape would indeed come to Upper Canada and be used for making wine that was usually deemed to be of rather poor quality. However, it is a mistake to associate the grape with Schiller. It seems more likely that Kathleen Hick's wording "eventually became" has been misinterpreted and does not refer to John Schiller at all but to Clinton grapes that would indeed be planted on Schiller's property, but only some 30 years after his death.

Equally anachronistic is the claim that Schiller supplied vines to France to save the French wine industry from the *Phylloxera* crisis that began half a century after his time. Vines from North America, including the Clinton, would eventually be used in the search for solutions to *Phylloxera*, but not vines from John Schiller!

Considering the number of erroneous claims and the lack of any contemporary evidence for either viticulture or winemaking on Schiller's part, it is no wonder that a scholar like Professor Hughes feels the story does not pass the "smell test." Yet, it would appear that, in spite of everything, the story is now rooted in our folklore. Schiller himself has been immortalized standing in front of his winery and barrels in a somewhat chauvinistic painting by William Biddle that was commissioned in the 1980's by the Canadian Wine Institute.

In the end we are left wanting to know more, not only about John Schiller, but also about the anonymous articles in the Toronto papers. It would be fascinating to know who wrote them and what their inspiration was, and to know more about their motivation to tell such a story at that particular moment in time.

Although mysteries remain, there is other information available about grapes and winemaking in Toronto Township—Cooksville in particular — that can be substantiated and that perhaps suggest some possible answers. It is interesting to note that in 1811, the year associated with Schiller, a man named William Custead, who had moved from Niagara to Toronto Township and was also a shoemaker, planted a nursery on a property just three miles east of Schiller's. In 1827 he published what is probably the first nursery catalogue in Upper Canada, a priceless document of which only one copy remains today (printed by William Lyon Mackenzie). He had agents selling his fruit trees and seeds from Niagara to Cobourg including eight different grapevines—vines which he had sourced from the Prince Nursery—including American hybrids like Bland's Virginia, and the Isabella, along with other varieties like Boston Sweet Water, Black Frontenac, and French Chocolate! Serving a rapidly growing market into the 1840s, Custead's nursery sold an amazing variety and number of fruit trees, as well as grapevines. More than likely, he sold his products to farmers in his own area, including perhaps the Parker family, who would become the owners of the original Schiller property. And we do know that by this time another nursery had opened in St. Catharines. It was operated by an American doctor named Chauncey Beadle. He was already experimenting with different grapes including the one that he preferred—the Isabella. Later, the son of Mr. Beadle would become involved with the winery that would be developed on the very property once homesteaded by John Schiller!

In the early 1840s in Cooksville itself, a retired British Vice-Admiral, Sir William George Parker, bought this property, which had changed hands several times in the interim since Schiller and moved his family there. Before long, work was started on a wonderful mansion which would be called Chateau Clair. Soon his sons, Henry and Melville, developed a farm including a vineyard which, according to Henry, had different vines including the Sweet Water eating grape and some American hybrids like the Clinton, which he described in a letter to a friend as "the hardiest of all that are useful." Henry's intent was to have a wine factory and, sure enough, in the mid 1860s he would open a winery on the property with the help of several other partners. We do not know if the Parkers found grapes already growing on the property; however, the story suggests that John Schiller's sons persevered with a vineyard. If there were grapes here, it would certainly help explain why a British family, presumably with little experience in growing grapes, would want to start a vineyard in Cooksville of all places! It is impossible now to discover what exactly was the motivation behind the effort that followed, but one thing is certain: it did not take long for Henry to become quite involved with grape growing and soon, winemaking. At that time such a surprising undertaking would indeed be considered "a rare thing."

The winery would remain in business through several owners down to the 1920's when winemaking in Cooksville finally came to an end. There was some renewed interest in the operation, but nothing came of it, and the property was sold for development after the mansion itself was destroyed by fire in 1934. Possibly this activity generated interest in the origins of the vineyard and winery on a property once owned by a man named Schiller, who was then assumed to have been the original vintner.

Unfortunately, it seems that we must be more content with the mystery of our vinous beginnings than with any solid fact, either that or wait until additional research is able to illuminate those early days of our history more clearly.

The Isabella: One "Prince" of a grape!

> The Catawba and the Isabella, with the Alexander, may certainly be considered the forerunners of the cultivated grapes of the species to which they belong (the fox or Labrusca type).
>
> —Hedrick, *The Grapes of New York,*
>
> Local patriotism favored the Isabella, which "soon became the cherished ornament and pride of every garden and door-yard".
>
> —Stiles, *A History of the City of Brooklyn*
>
> I do not offer any grapevines for sale except the Isabella. This is the only one that has borne fruit with me that I now recommend.
>
> —Beadle, *The St. Catharines Journal,* 1845

Following the Alexander—and most likely discovered earlier than the Catawba (certainly named earlier!)—was a third chance hybrid that would become a mainstay of American viticulture; that is, until the Concord took centre stage. Named the Isabella, it is a black grape with large, well-formed clusters and an abundant flavor that shows the musky or foxy nature of *labrusca* parentage. Its specific origin is unknown, but it is generally credited to the area of Dorchester, South Carolina. U.P. Hedrick, writing long after the time, believed it originated some time in the 18th century, probably in one of the Carolinas, and that it was cultivated in many widely separated neighbourhoods prior to 1800. It appears to be a random pollination of a wild *labrusca* vine and a Burgundy vine possibly introduced by Huguenots who had settled in South Carolina in the 1760's.

In1816 this new grape was introduced into New York by a merchant from Brooklyn named Colonel George Gibbs. With the involvement of Mrs. Isabella Gibbs, George's wife, the grape reached the attention and hands of William R. Prince, member of a well-known family of nurserymen at the Linnaean Gardens in Flushing on Long Island. William, who was just 21 years old at the time, was developing a keen interest in grapes. He saw the Isabella as a potential rival to the Catawba and decided that this grape deserved a name. What better than to name it in honour of Mrs. Isabella Gibbs, and to introduce it as such to the world! And as the Isabella, this hybrid grape soon developed a following in Ohio and New York State.

Nicholas Longworth planted Isabella grapes as early as 1823 and made wine from them as well as from Alexander grapes, but it was the Catawba that would make him quit his law practice. In 1824 Elijah Fay planted both Catawba and Isabella near Brocton, New York, the beginning of what would become the famous Chatauqua grape belt along Lake Erie. Shortly after, both Isabella and Catawba grapes were brought to the Finger Lakes, and planted in Hammondsport by the Reverend William Bostwick in 1829 as the beginning of a nascent grape and wine industry in that region.

More than likely the Isabella came to the Niagara region around the same time. We have already noted that William Custead, who was operating a Nursery in Toronto Township, in Upper Canada, had listed Isabella in his catalogue among his eight varieties of grapes in 1827, a fact that illustrates how quickly the popularity of this grape had grown, no doubt due to the efforts of the Linnaean Garden and of William Prince, who himself had made wine from the Isabella, a wine which he described as "of excellent quality ... met with the approbation of some of the most accurate judges in our country."

In 1830 Prince began the breeding of grapes in America, growing 10,000 seedlings "from admixture under every variety of circumstance" in order to develop his own hybrid grape that would combine the hardiness and immunities of the native American species but with the more acceptable wine flavours of the *vinifera*. To accompany this work, he wrote a booklet entitled *Treatise on the Vine,* which featured a drawing of the Isabella grape on the front page. The booklet contained descriptions of over 200 foreign and 80 American varieties; it was a considerable achievement, providing much historical information and organization of many grape varieties at that time and marking him as a recognized expert on American viticulture.

Shortly afterwards, Dr. William W. Valk, a fellow inhabitant of Flushing, developed what is considered to be the first successful, deliberate man-made inter-specific hybrid by crossing the Isabella with the *vinifera* Black Hamburg, producing a grape known as 'Ada' that was exhibited in 1852 at a meeting of the American Pomological Society in Philadelphia. But it was the Isabella, along with the Catawba, that would lead to the evolution of a commercial winemaking industry in the Northern States.

Its fame spread quickly as far as Europe, where it was introduced early on, and even to Russia, where it is still widely grown; its musky flavour reminding the people there of the smell of bedbugs! To others, both the Ada and the Catawba would suggest strawberries, a characteristic due to the *labrusca* component in the cross. Hedrick has suggested that it was probably the arrival of the Isabella in Europe before 1830 that resulted in the introduction of *Phylloxera*; however, actual proof of this is lacking.

As a winemaking grape, the Isabella was often criticized for its low sugar content. For sufficient alcohol content, wine from the Isabella grapes required added sugar, and was thus considered "unnatural," and as a grape incapable of producing "fine" wine. Yet it proved to be an extremely significant import to Upper Canada—one of the first hybrids brought from New York State to the St. Catharines area. An American physician, Dr. Chauncey Beadle, had moved here in 1821 and a few years later, in the early 1830s, he became proprietor of the St. Catharines Nursery, a 100 acre site on Geneva Street near Russell Avenue. Like William Custead, Beadle first became an important cultivator of fruit trees, declaring in 1839 that he had not less than 250,000 available. His *Catalogue of Fruit Trees, Cultivated and for Sale at the St. Catharines Nursery,* published in 1841, is still available to be read.

On October 9, 1845, Beadle advertised in the St. Catharines Journal that he had Isabella grapes for sale at 1s3d each. He stated that he had acquired them from the plantings of Judge Jesse Buel, a highly-esteemed agricultural reformer from Albany, New York, and implied that he had tried to grow others that would not bear fruit. He also noted that he would send out free catalogues upon request! From that time on, more and more individuals gained an interest in grapes. Grapes began to appear with increasing frequency at Agricultural Fairs, a significant step forward on the way to grape growing on a commercial scale.

We can thank Chauncey Beadle along with his son, Delos White Beadle (who carried on the nursery after his father's death in 1863), for their inspirational and motivational efforts in horticultural activity and for the planting of grapes. Their efforts led, in no small degree, to much of the progress and development of fruit growing in this part of the province.

And though it is impossible to say that the Isabella was the first grape to come to the area from south of the border, it was certainly the first grape to draw serious attention to the planting of grapes in the area, and as such it deserves to be recognized for its historical importance to our grape and wine industries.

Clearly, the Isabella—which would one day be planted from Upper Canada to Europe, to Africa, to the Balkans, and even to Fiji—had become accepted as a very hardy and worthwhile variety. However, although it is still grown as close by as New York State today and is still made as a commercial wine, it has long since lost favour in Ontario and is no longer available here.

From brewing and distilling in early Niagara to ... fermenting!

Grapes have succeeded well in the Niagara district.

—Robert Gourlay, 1817

The Isabella grapevine stands the winter well ... I have raised this year, from two stocks, not over 5 years old, two bushels ... I have no hesitation in believing that the grape might be cultivated in this district to a great extent and be profitable to the raiser.

—William Woodruff, 1846

The same decade (1850's) also saw the beginnings of commercial grape growing and winemaking ... a significant increase in the numbers involved in the nascent grape and wine industry.

—Hughes, *The World of Niagara Wine*, 2013.

The success of fruit culture in this Province which has followed may be said to be greatly due to the efforts of these few men (Fruit Growers' Association) more than to any other agency.

—Smith, *50 Years of Peach Culture in Ontario*

After the War of 1812-1814, life in Niagara was able to continue on a somewhat more peaceful footing what with the British still in control, and given the emergence of a new national pride among the somewhat sparse settlers, who had helped fend off an American invasion with odds of 14 to 1 in the Americans' favour. And now, with growing immigration, progress occurred rapidly, especially where communities enjoyed the advantage of a winning location. The early Village of Twelve on the Twelve Mile Creek in 1827 had only 400 inhabitants, but when it was incorporated in 1845 as St. Catharines and, after the development of the original Welland Canal, the population increased to 3400 people, and it became the most important centre in the Niagara Peninsula. Other villages along the route from Stamford (Niagara Falls) to Hamilton, including Beamsville, Grimsby, and Stoney Creek, would also blossom as early farming communities. Grimsby, for example, would become known as the 'Peach Garden of Canada' due largely to the efforts of Andrew Smith and Charles Woolverton and to the arrival in 1853 of the Great Western Railway.

Many of the first arrivals in the area had brought seeds and plants with them from their previous homes in the United States, and they found decent soils and a favourable climate for their agricultural endeavours, truly a necessity of life. Before long, grapevines—now becoming more available thanks to the efforts of men like Pierre Legaux, William Prince, and soon John Adlum—would make their way here as a potential source of grape wine, successor to the ciders and fruit wines that were no doubt familiar to many of the immigrants. Still, homemade wine was much less available and certainly less popular than whiskey and beer, which were inexpensive and readily available from the numerous distilleries and breweries that had sprung up in many of the settlements. Although information is difficult to come by, some records give insight into these early operations. In Grimsby, for example, there is mention in a lease dated August 11, 1823 of a distillery owned by Henry Nelles. As well, it is known that two distilleries were selling whiskey for one shilling a quart, with Grimsby beer offered at one pound ten shillings a barrel! One of the three distilleries in Chippewa by the Niagara River could produce 1200 gallons of whiskey a day, making it the foremost distillery in all of Upper Canada. With whiskey and beer so cheap and life so difficult, it is no wonder that alcohol came to play such a significant role in the everyday life of so many people in the developing communities.

Within 15 years of the ending of the war of 1812-1814, access to several American hybrid grapes was further facilitated by their arrival in nurseries like that of William Custead in Toronto Township—who was selling them with the help of agents from East of Toronto to Niagara certainly by 1827—and the St. Catharines Nursery of Dr. Beadle. In short order, this availability would stimulate an interest in growing grapes for home/farm winemaking, as well as for table use. The survey conducted by Robert Gourlay suggests that some form of plantings took place as early as 1817. Unfortunately, he failed to provide any information about the variety of grapes, or their source, or who was growing them. But such documents clearly show that the roots of grape growing in this area can be traced back some two centuries to the early 1800's.

One of the first families to become involved with viticulture in the Beamsville area was that of John and Nancy Kilborn. John was born in New Hampshire in 1772 and moved to Connecticut where he married Nancy Melinda Hubbard in 1795. In Vermont they had the first of their six children, then moved north to Beamsville in Clinton Township, Lincoln County in 1820 where they continued to add to the family. Their second child— Rowley Kilborn (1800-1880), who married Kezia Corwin, grand-daughter of Beamsville founder Jacob Beam, in 1825—is credited with planting the first grapes here, supposedly a red variety. Could "Rowley's Red" have been an Alexander? Or an Isabella? In all likelihood, we probably will never know for sure, but the Kilborn name would continue to be associated with grapes for some time.

The Kilborns had moved north to Upper Canada at a time when grape fever was just catching on in the United States, thanks, in particular, to the development of the Catawba and the Isabella, and to the possibility of a winemaking industry that was about to become a reality. Although the history of failure with European *viniferas* might have caused skepticism, these hybrids offered considerable hope; it would take more than a border to stop them from catching the interest of local people. Upper Canada would prove receptive territory for the new vines, a territory where there had been no disappointing experiences yet with *vinifera* grapes to dampen any emerging enthusiasm.

At this time public interest in agriculture in general began to be stimulated when the Colonial Government passed an act in 1820 to encourage the establishment of agricultural societies. This was followed in 1830 by a public act to further encourage agriculture, in which the governor was authorized to pay 100 pounds to any district agricultural society that could raise a subscription of 50 pounds on its own. By 1830 half a dozen societies were active in places like York, Kingston, and the Newcastle district with exhibitions of farm produce that gave cash prizes as rewards. With the population swelling now to almost 200,000, the growing of wheat gained primacy on farms. Within a few years, improved farm implements and labour-saving machinery would be developed to help with the needs of a growing population. In August of 1846 the first province-wide association, the Upper Canada Agricultural Society, came into being with 297 paid subscriptions. It was followed by the first provincial exhibition in Toronto in October. The exhibition was complete with a ploughing match and banquet for the executives and for the elite of Toronto! Exhibitions would be held annually in major port cities like Toronto, Hamilton, Kingston, Brockville, and Cobourg, eventually settling in one city, Toronto, as the now famous Canadian National Exhibition.

With the increasing diversification of agriculture in the province, other societies evolved. The numbers increased from 22 in 1852 to 61 in 1859. These included associations concerned more specifically with fruit and grapes, such as the County of Lincoln Grape Growers' Association and the Fruit Growers' Association of Upper Canada, which was started in 1858 by a small group of keen horticulturists and farmers to increase awareness of the province's potential as a fruit-growing region. The initial meeting took place at a Judge Campbell's home and included Dr. Beadle of St. Catharines, a Reverend Burnett and Judge Logie both of Hamilton, and Grimsby farmers Charles Woolverton and Andrew Smith. The association was formally organized with Judge Campbell as first president on January 19, 1859. Much of the formative learning about grape growing and winemaking was developed at these early meetings where information would be shared about such issues as the usefulness of particular grape varieties and the basic formula for making wine.

By this time, grapes had already appeared at the Niagara Agricultural Semi-Annual Fair at St. Catharines and, in 1846, judges for the fair commended William Woodruff for his exhibit of the cultivation of Isabella grapes. Woodruff's response is noted at the beginning of this chapter. Obviously, these early references to the growing of Isabella grapes in Niagara concerned grapes that were experimental more than commercial, but it would not be long before grapes like the Isabella and the Clinton and other 'new' varieties including the Delaware, the Diana, and the Concord—all sourced from the United States—would be planted throughout Canada West.

Numerous individuals whose names appear in various exhibitions and fairs were exhibiting grapes and winning prizes for their efforts, an indication that grapes were now widely planted in the Niagara Peninsula, including the area around Hamilton and then east around Lake Ontario. The 1855 Provincial Exhibition held in Cobourg, named as winners both black grapes and white grapes from Niagara, Belleville, Peterborough, Ameliasburg, and Toronto. A significantly varied bunch!

In the 1850s, John Corwin Kilborn, son of Rowley and Kezia Kilborn, acquired a property of 17 acres on Ontario Street in Beamsville and soon became a prominent farm winemaker. He was busy in Grimsby as well (several of his family were married and living there) planting a vine in 1854 that within three years had covered a 40 square foot trellis, producing some 1200 clusters of grapes. In 1860 he reported that he had produced four or five barrels of wine from the vine in 1857 and was able to sell his wine for $1.75 a gallon with the comment "it is worth four times as much as the miserable stuff sold by our merchants under the name of wine." In 1862 John won a $3 prize at the Provincial exhibition in Toronto for the 'best grape wine' and two years later in a letter to "The Canada Farmer" he declared: "I have a hobby—my hobby is the grape ... I have growing in my garden 30 varieties of grapes ... the only difficulty in growing grapes in Canada has been in obtaining varieties that would ripen sufficiently early. Of the 30 varieties I am cultivating, there is one that stands thus far unrivalled as to quality, and which, tested by the saccharometer, is as sweet or sweeter than any European variety. I mean the Delaware." John would not be the only one to highly praise this particular grape, another inter-specific hybrid that had only recently become available

Comments like these, reflecting the opinions of early growers and amateur winemakers (amateur signifying a true passion for winemaking) provide invaluable insight into the nature of an industry in its infancy. In a region where only wild grapes could be found just half a century earlier, the importation of hybrid vines, though at first few and far between, had produced important results by the 1840's. Then, one has to be impressed by how quickly grapes like the Delaware and some of the others that Kilborn mentions made their way into Canada West and especially by the number of different vines John was attempting to grow at this rather early time in our grape history. His was a true passion for growing grapes and turning them into wine, and he deserves to be acknowledged as an important precursor in this industry that would soon set down roots.

Indeed, these were exciting times with the population increasing (by 1867 "Canada" would have almost 3.5 million people), transportation opening up, especially by rail after 1853, and with the arrival of the industrial age and a company like Massey becoming the leading manufacturer of new agricultural implements. Four out of every five people were farmers, yet the country was well on the way to moving from pioneer society to a Victorian society. Still, life was difficult, especially given the unpredictable availability of basics like food and water, and given epidemic diseases like smallpox, typhoid, and diphtheria. All things considered, it is no wonder that many people turned to alcohol for solace. Indeed, the per capita consumption was already at four gallons. Of course, little of what was consumed was wine, and even less was local wine.

But by the end of the 1850s, with several grapes blessed with winemaking potential now available, it was inevitable that someone, following John Kilborn's lead, would seize the opportunity and take winemaking itself to a true commercial level.

A plethora of new vines, both discovered 'by chance' and others 'man-made': but not all grapes are created equal!

> Farmers' periodicals and newspapers from the Niagara Peninsula do not mention grapes until 1850, when it was suggested that two new varieties called Isabella and Catawba would be likely to succeed in Canada.
>
> —Masson, *Wine from Ontario Grapes*, 1979

Introducing grapes to Upper Canada and Ontario: 1790-1880

> The 1860's were the years of a "grape boom," years in which the acreage of vines in New York, Ohio, and Missouri increased at geometrical rates, when wineries were opened to take advantage of the new production, when new varieties were introduced almost daily to an eager public caught up in what the papers called the "grape mania."
>
> —Pinney *A History of Wine in America.*

> I think production of new varieties of grapes is in its infancy, and that we will yet be able to introduce new varieties to rival the French grapes, and enable us to produce more wine to the acre than they can in France—in fact we can almost do so now.
>
> —Haskins, *Ontario Agricultural Commission Report*, 1881.

> About 1880, however, by the introduction of the Niagara grape, a strong stimulus was given to the grape industry. Vines of this variety were sold at $1.25 apiece and the purchaser was bound to sell all the wood from these vines to the company and was not allowed to plant a single cutting, under a heavy penalty.
>
> —Revett, *Department of Agriculture Bulletin*, 1912.

When people talk about "wild" or "native" grapes, those indigenous to eastern North America, the impression is sometimes given that all such grapes are the same: well-adapted to their environment and able to grow over a very wide area but with a chemistry and flavour profile that means any winemaking from them is a waste of time. The history of American winemaking does provide many examples of people with negative comments about the taste and quality of 'local' wines and only a few positive ones (and the motivation for these comments are of a questionable nature). But not all wild grapes are the same, a fact recorded by the earliest colonists who noted differences in size, shape, colour, sweetness, taste, as well as the nature of the vine, its growing location, and its time of ripening. Today the various grapes are known to us as species whose names reflect these various differences. The species most often associated with the first

American hybrids is *Vitis labrusca,* the oldest known American species, named by Linnaeus in 1763 as simply the "wild grape," but which the colonists identified as the 'northern fox grape' (or sometimes the 'skunk' grape) as a result of its unforgettable, musky character. The species which over time seems to have made the "best" local wine, *Vitis rotundifolia,* also had a distinctive flavour which earned it the name Southern Fox (or muscadine), although the flavour was different from its northern cousin. The colonists noted its round shape, hence its species name, and sometimes referred to it as the 'bullet' grape for this reason. Unlike *Vitis labrusca,* this grape does not hybridize readily with other species. Nor is it significant in any discussion of grapes in what would become Ontario.

Another very common species, *Vitis riparia,* was often found along river banks (ripa: river bank) as its Latin name suggests. Its small berries were not used often for winemaking, but today its tough, resistant rootstock and its hardiness to cold makes it an ideal parent in various newer American hybrids. Some species show much less of the foxy character than others, for example *Vitis aestivalis,* the 'summer' grape, and some do not grow up around trees, like *Vitis rupestris,* the sand grape, also called the beach, rock, mountain, and bush grape, while a grape like *Vitis cordifolia,* the raccoon, chicken, or winter grape, made such harsh wine that it required the addition of brandy to make it palatable. In North America there are over 20 such species, a number which offered great hope for local winemaking in the early days of settlement, a hope that went unfulfilled, because the wine they made was a disappointment. However, without some of these grapes, there would have been no inter-specific hybrids involving the imported *Vitis vinifera* and no resulting improvement in grape quality.

After the discovery of the first hybrids, the Alexander, Bland, Catawba, and Isabella, at least three additional "chance" hybrids would make their appearance before 1850, all proving to be viticulturally worthwhile, as well as providing potential for winemaking. Moreover, during this period the thought occurred to a number of individuals that if Mother Nature could create such vines on her own, how much more might man himself achieve by controlling the desirable qualities of each parent in the mix? Thus began the science of hybridizing grapes as "grape scientists," through deliberate experimentation, produced crosses between varieties of the same species and between different species in an effort to provide better grapes for North Eastern America. The objective was, of course, to achieve in the new vine less sensitivity to the climate and more resistance to diseases, along with a better wine quality, as well as to obtain an optimal balance of native and *vinifera* qualities in the offspring. Reference has already been made to William Prince's work with seedlings and the development of the Ada by Dr. William Valk—some of the earliest work in grape breeding here.

What ensued after the early 1840s was a remarkable proliferation of new man-made vines, first with straightforward primary hybrids (the crossing of two vines of the same or different species), then with secondary hybrids (using already existing hybrids with a *vinifera* parent), and then with much more complex hybridizing. In spite of the exceptional interest in grape breeding and viticulture, very few of these efforts would result in real success stories; yet eventually a wine industry would develop based on a number of these hybrids, and the industry would be welcomed and appreciated.

In the 1820s and 1830s another grape came to the fore with different stories attached to its discovery. According to an August 1867 article in *The Cultivator and Country Gentleman*, the Clinton grape, a spontaneous hybrid of *labrusca* and *riparia,* was developed when a man named Hugh White transplanted a vine he found in Whiteboro, New York, to a plot at Hamilton College in Clinton, New York where he was a student. Some accept this version of the discovery; however, there is no evidence that Hugh named the grape or that he disseminated it. Others believe that a man named Samuel Freeman, of Saratoga, New York, discovered a grape in 1831 and sent the grapes and cuttings to a friend, one Lyman Langworthy of Rochester. Lyman grafted a cutting on a wild "frost" grape rootstock and then propagated it. He then named it after Governor Clinton of New York. By 1835 it was in the hands of others, and it soon made its way to the Cooksville area in Upper Canada.

About this time, Nicholas Longworth wrote in a letter to H. Watts of New Jersey that he had experimented with the Clinton, making two versions, one of which involved the addition of 17 ounces of sugar to a gallon that he found to be of "fine flavor." The other he made with the skins on and without sugar. This version turned out quite acidic and low in alcohol. However, at the same time he ordered more grapes as well as 2000 to 5000 cuttings! Through time, others would comment on Clinton's wine with a general lack of appreciation, describing it as "sour" or "unpleasant." Some

40 years later, in the 1881 report of the Ontario Agricultural Commission, Mr. W. Haskins, the grape-growing City Engineer from Hamilton, would comment: "There is a peculiarity about wine made from Clinton grapes. It makes excellent wine but it requires a few years to mature it. It holds so much acid in solution that it requires a longer time to precipitate it."

As has been the case with grapes and wine, undoubtedly from the very beginning of time, there has been controversy and differences of opinion. This will be true for many of the 'new' vines, as some grew better in some locations than others or produced better quality grapes in certain years. But the Clinton, closer to a native grape than most hybrids, did play a significant role in our history; and it would prove to be an important rootstock later in helping to remedy the *Phylloxera* crisis in Europe.

Another important chance hybrid known as the Delaware came to prominence sometime in the 1840s in Delaware County, Ohio, after a discovery that can only be deemed a mystery. An unknown farmer was said to have brought forward a vine originally found in New Jersey a number of years earlier. He cultivated it and in 1853 gave some grapes to fellow horticulturist Abram Thompson, publisher of the *Delaware Gazette*. Thompson sent grapes to the Massachusetts Horticultural Society in 1855. They were amazed at the grape. They gave him a silver goblet in recognition and commissioned a life-size oil painting of Thompson, which they gave to his wife. The Delaware was further developed by another horticulturalist named George Campbell, who then sold the grape world-wide. The grape demonstrates characteristics of both *vinifera* and native American species, but there is disagreement whether the latter is *labrusca* or *aestivalis*. The grapes are smallish and pink in colour, and they produce a wine with an intriguing, spicy taste but, lacking foxiness, these grapes are the least *labrusca*-like of all these early grapes. It quickly became the grape of choice for many individuals. Numerous comments indicated that it was an early grape that always ripened well and produced abundantly with excellent sugar levels (unlike most other American hybrids), and that it made a good native wine that was able to compete favourably with any import.

Nicholas Longworth, writing in a letter to Mr. Ellwanger, declared that a sample of wine from the Delaware grape "was the best wine he ever made, possessed more body, was a heavier wine, and a better wine than any other that he had tasted." Considering the success that he had enjoyed with the Catawba grape, this is no faint praise! Certainly the qualities of the Delaware for winemaking were quickly appreciated, and it was widely planted during the 1850s and 1860s. It also proved to be a very popular grape in Canada West, growing successfully from Niagara to Ottawa. The opinion of the previously mentioned Mr. Haskins, as recorded in the *Ontario Agricultural Commission Report of 1881*, says it all: "After reading all I could on the subject and making personal inspection of some of the vineyards in Canada, I came to the conclusion that the best grape for winemaking was the Delaware. This grape is very free from what is called the 'fox' ... what we mean by the foxy grape is a mousey flavour, such as may be tasted in the Concord and the Clinton (the smell of a cup in which a mouse has been). The Delaware is also very free from disease."

Other hybrids came fast and furious. One hybrid, the Diana, was grown for a time in Ontario, and became a rival to the Delaware. The Diana was associated with a lady named Mrs. Diana Crehore who propagated it in a town called Milton, Massachusetts and exhibited it in 1843 at the Massachusetts Horticultural Society. The grape, which ripened consistently with appropriate sugar levels, was described as the "first seedling American grape," possibly a seedling of Catawba. An interesting comment on the grape comes from the aforementioned Mr. Ellwanger, who wrote the following about the grape in 1853: "Diana, also, will beyond doubt make a fine wine, for it is sweet. There is not any of that fibre which is in the most of our native grapes, and which when pressed is very sour, and needs sugar. In my opinion Diana and Delaware are the only two grapes which will here make a really fine wine. They are strong growers and their fruit will hang upon the vines for a long time after ripening."

However, as well-liked as these grapes were, the most important hybrid of them all, the one grape that became more highly valued and more widely planted than any other, and yet at the same time more pilloried and vilified for winemaking than any other, would be the Concord!

Hudson Cattell, author of *The Wines of the East*, introduces his comments on the Concord grape this way: "In purely commercial terms, the introduction of the Concord grape in the early 1850s was perhaps the single most important development in Eastern viticulture in the 19th century." Ephriam Wales Bull was born in Concord, Massachusetts in 1805 and grew up among grapes in the Hudson Valley. In 1840 he returned to Concord and bought a house he named Grapevine Cottage that was down the road from the Emerson, Thoreau, Hawthorne, and Alcott homesteads. The story goes that some boys had found wild grapes on his property by the river, and that Bull used these grapes to create some seedlings three years later in 1843. One of these produced a grapevine with remarkable fruit ... and thus the Concord was born! It was shown at the Massachusetts Horticultural Society in 1852 and, in 1853, it won first prize at the Boston Horticultural Society Exhibition. By 1854 it was being offered for sale at the amazing price of five dollars a vine. In spite of the price, the Concord spread quickly throughout the country reaching Chautauqua County in New York State in 1856. In 1865 it was named the "best grape for cultivation," a title it held for over 100 years. Bull himself thought that the seeds of a New England fox (*labrusca*) grape were probably accidentally crossed by the pollen of a nearby Catawba, but the truth of the genesis of the grape may never be known. Mr. Bull did make some money from his creation early on through the efforts of Hovey & Company, the leading nursery in Boston, but unhappily he died in poverty at the age of 90, while other individuals would go on to create fortunes using Concord for making grape juice (and to a lesser extent jams, jellies, and pies) as well as Concord grape wine. His epitaph records the reality: "He sowed, but others reaped!"

The catalogue of the company described the grape as follows: "This remarkably fine new American variety is the greatest acquisition that has ever yet been made to our hardy grapes ... sufficiently hardy to withstand the coldest climate, and early enough to mature its fruit in any part of the Northern or New England States ... and the berries have never been known to mildew, rot, and drop off, under any circumstances during the five years since it has first borne fruit." And so North America became Concord country, and the name Concord became eponymous for grape—this purebred *labrusca*, as Thomas Pinney says "without a suspicion of *vinifera* genes," foxy in the extreme, with a flavour, aroma, and identity that generations of people have come to accept as their standard for "grape-ness." Growers would come to love it for its productivity and its adaptability to a wide variety of growing conditions. Dr. Welch and millions of people would love it for its unfermented juice. And, although it would dominate commercial vineyards eventually in Ontario, the wine it made would condemn the entire industry when consumers eventually sought out the more elegant and complex wines produced solely from *Vitis vinifera*.

In 1856 Edward Stanford Rogers of Salem, Massachusetts began introducing his crosses of *vinifera* and native grapes. A nursery catalogue of about 1862 tells us that Rogers crossed a wild *labrusca* grape called Mammoth Globe with Black Hamburg and Chasselas to produce several new varieties. His work was considered a special achievement by many, "a conquest over nature—a new era in American grape culture ... His grapes are considered to be but little inferior, if at all, to those of Europe." All in all there were at least 18 successful creations, most only numbered, as in #15, a light amber, aromatic and vigorous grape that would later be called Agawam, one of his most popular grapes. Several of his varieties including #9 (Lindley) and #22 (Salem), as well as Agawam, would be brought to Ontario where, over a period of time, they were welcomed by growers.

Inspired by the work of Rogers, many other individuals became involved in grape breeding and this was accompanied by a tremendous interest in viticulture that would spill over into Canada West. One success was a grape named Hartford Prolific. The Hartford was the result of a cross between a *labrusca* and the Isabella. It would be planted as early as 1862 in Port Dalhousie by a man named William Read. Others would try growing it in the1860s and 1870s. Interestingly, it does not seem to have been popular in the United States.

In Missouri, Jacob Rommel was creating hybrids of *labrusca* and *riparia* that would resist disease and the cold winters of the Midwest. One of his seedlings became known as Elvira; this white grape would become economically very important in Ontario.

Other hybridizers were now beginning to produce second and third generation crosses, thus adding to an extensive list of new grapes that would attract the interest and attention of numerous individuals and farmers. For example, a man named Jacob Moore of Brighton, New York, would produce the first 'secondary' American hybrid by crossing the Diana with the Concord (which became very popular as a 'parent' in many crosses) to produce a grape called Brighton; this was a red-coloured grape of good quality that also came to be widely planted in Ontario.

And Andrew Jackson Caywood, a commercial nurseryman in New York, would develop perhaps the most successful white grape for quality winemaking. He named it Dutchess. It was a hybrid of possibly four different species: *vinifera, labrusca, bourquinia,* and *aestivalis. Although the grape was never widely planted in Ontario, Dutchess would be made as a varietal wine by a number of wineries including Charal, London Winery, and Inniskillin into the 1980's.*

Helping create grapes that would grow successfully throughout Ontario, a man named Charles Arnold, following the lead of many others south of the border, began to hybridize new grapes in Paris, Ontario. Born in Bedfordshire, England in 1818, Arnold moved to what would become #2 Arnold St. in Paris, built a house in the 1840's and by 1853 had established the Paris Nurseries. By 1868 he was offering grapevines for sale by mail, promoting "the largest and best assortment of hardy grapes ever offered by an nurseryman in Canada ... all the new varieties of merit including all the best of the recent Roger's Hybrids, #15, #3, #4, and #19, at $1 each or 12 for $10."

Arnold created at least five new grapes of his own from crosses of the Clinton and the Black St. Peters, including one white grape named Autochon and four black grapes, Cornucopia, Brant, Canada, and Othello. The Canada and the Brant received favorable comments in *The Canada Farmer*, while the Othello, which was distributed to members of the Fruit Growers' Association of Ontario in 1874, was considered a late ripener. For his work with grapes, other fruits, wheat, corn, and peas, Arnold was acclaimed "Canada's greatest hybridist." At the Centennial Exhibition in 1876 he received a medal and diploma for his new hybrids. He died at age 65 in 1893.

Several others would emulate Arnold's work and attempt to develop grapes that would grow or produce better. These hybridizers or nurserymen were the likes of Delos Beadle of St. Catharines and W.H. Read of Port Dalhousie, who himself created several new grapes including Ontario, Silver Cluster, Moyer, Lincoln, Jessica, and Chippewa. Other important work was done by men like Peter C. Dempsey of Albury, and W.H. Mills and William Haskins of Hamilton. However, their best creations, named Burnet, Mills, and Abyssinia, while popular for a while, were eventually discarded because of susceptibility to mildew or lack of hardiness. This was the fate shared by most of the grapes hybridized locally.

While this work was taking place in Ontario, just across the border in Lockport, New York, a man named Claudius C. Hoag had started a nursery

Introducing grapes to Upper Canada and Ontario: 1790-1880

on his farm. There in 1866 he cross-pollinated seeds from the Concord grape with the Cassady, a very hardy white grape. Ten of the seeds sprouted. In 1867 he transplanted them. One seed showed unusual vigour. By 1873 he had his first fruit—large, greenish-yellow grapes with a strong musky perfume, reminding some of jasmine flowers. The grape was immediately successful and was quickly planted in New York State vineyards. A circular from 1881 stated that the vines would not be sold but would instead given to any grower who would remit one-half of the net sales to the Niagara White Grape Company. Vines were sent all over the world, flooding the market. By 1921 the company would disappear, but not the grape, named Niagara, which was heavily planted in Ontario after 1882. Unfortunately, with its strong foxy character, it would prove to be disappointing as a source of dry white table wine—a flaw that would doom it a century later, along with its Concord parent, to vinous infamy in spite of its popularity as an eating grape.

There are abundant references to other hybridized grapes in private letters, the minutes of various agricultural and horticultural societies, the occasional book on the subject, and in nursery catalogues, sometimes with descriptions of their growing habits, their appearance and flavours, their time of ripening, sugar levels, their susceptibility to various plant diseases, and whether they made decent wine. Unfortunately, these comments are about all that remains of the majority of them. They have disappeared in the mists of time, overshadowed by those hybrids which performed better.

By the end of the 19th century, literally thousands of hybrids would be developed; yet it is significant that most would prove to be unacceptable for winemaking. Ironically, the small number of "chance" or "spontaneous" hybrids, created naturally and discovered by various individuals, would provide the real foundation of both the American and Ontario wine industries and would be the grapes for the majority of our wines well into the 20th century.

Clearly, in spite of man's best efforts and "grape mania," not all grapes were created equal!

The 1860s: A commercial grape and wine industry is "born" - but whose baby is it?

> It is almost impossible to get any definite idea of the early days of the grape in the Niagara District...In 1858 Mr. W. Kitchen and Mr. J.R. Pettit planted some grapes at Grimsby.
>
> —Revett, *Ontario Department of Agriculture Bulletin #202,* from the Annual Report of the Fruit Branch, 1909

> The early winemakers, a number of whom were looking toward the establishment of a wine industry, approached their hobbies with sincerity and a true desire to improve the art. At meetings of agriculturists they discussed methods and formulae ... Most of the discussion at those early meetings centred around the desirability of the numerous grape varieties that were being grown.
>
> — Rannie, *Wines of Ontario.*

> What we do know about the last half of the nineteenth century is that winemaking was in a slow transition from something farmers did for their own household consumption into a more formal and growing industry...At some point the actual industry emerged, but it is difficult to set a date and point precisely at one event that indicated the transition.
>
> —Malleck, *The World of Niagara Wine,* 2013.

Stepping back in time to find the beginning of something is challenging, often simply because of a lack of information, and often because the historical data, even when it can be located, proves to be questionable, or clouded by romance or by someone's particular bias. This makes it difficult to sort out fact from fancy. As far as the beginnings of our grape and wine industry are concerned, the stories of Johann Schiller (lack of credible evidence) and Porter Adams (erroneously credited with being our first commercial grape grower due to a badly-worded statement by Mr. Revett in Bulletin

#202 cited above) are good examples of this. Indeed, in his article in "The World of Niagara Wine," Dan Malleck warns that "it is important to be aware of the limitations of the oft-repeated stories regarding the origins of the industry."

Fortunately we do have good information: newspaper articles and advertisements, records from various associations, private letters, and government documents, which all help significantly in delineating the genesis of our grape and wine industry that occurred shortly before Confederation. From these records it has become clear that there was no sudden 'birth' of either commercial grape-growing or commercial winemaking, and that no single individual can be deemed responsible for the arrival of either industry. Both grape growing and winemaking evolved over a period of some 20 years through the efforts of many individuals in different locations, beginning with small-scale viticulture and amateur winemakers who created wines from the new grapes, either for their own use or for competitions at various exhibitions or, as in John Kilborn's case, for sale to a willing buyer. Thus, to speak of "a father" of either industry—as has been done for some time now—while historically interesting, is really not history as we should understand it.

During the late 1850s and into the 1860s more extensive plantings of American hybrid grapes in a number of locations led directly to the making of native wines on a larger scale. The names of some of these growers were reported in two early-twentieth-century government bulletins: number 202 (1909) by T.B. Revett, and number 237 (1916) by F.M Clement. The bulletins included the names of the grapes they planted. In addition to Kitchen and Pettit in Grimsby, they mention William Read of Port Dalhousie, who planted three acres of Concord, Hartford Prolific, and Delaware in 1862, as well as Peter Wright of Stamford (Niagara Falls), who planted three acres of Isabella in the same year. In 1863, Mr. Lusee, on the mountain near Winona, and J.M. Stewart, Henry Lottridge, and Christopher Biggar, below the mountain, planted small vineyards. Five years later Mr. F.G. Stewart of Stamford, planted 2 ½ acres of Concord and Delaware and Mr. P. Prest, also in Stamford, planted an acre of Delaware, Concord and Hartford Prolific. Finally, in 1869 Mr. Lowin of St. David's planted two acres of Concord.

As we shall see in later chapters, by 1850 grapes had already been extensively planted in Cooksville by the Parker family. As well, a 13-acre vineyard just outside Hamilton was started about 1859 by William Haskins (Chief Engineer for the City of Hamilton) and significant vineyards were established on Pelee Island (then called Point au Pelee) in the late 1860s by a number of individuals intent on making wine. Ontario, as the new province of Canada would soon be called, was witnessing a tremendous development in commercial fruit growing and grapes, both for eating and for winemaking. Soon, the industry spread from southern Ontario through to the Niagara Peninsula from Hamilton to Stamford, and on to the north shore of Lake Ontario through Cooksville and Toronto.

The first two attempts at serious industrial wine production happened virtually at the same time in Canada West just prior to its becoming Ontario. These attempts were well documented. The one was essentially an individual effort in the Niagara Peninsula; the other was an effort by a consortium of grape and wine enthusiasts in Cooksville, just to the west of Toronto. One might choose either of the parties as our first commercial winery, as both parties had planted a suitable vineyard prior to 1860. However, the evidence for the first commercial winery appears to favour a cattle breeder and fruit grower named William Whitney Kitchen, whose wine-making operations had been started in the early 1860s in Grimsby, Canada West.

The Kitchen name was already prominent in early 19th century Grimsby when William Whitney Kitchen was born, but his birth on April 22, 1824 actually occurred in Dumfries Township, Brant County. His grandfather, also William (1761-1813), had married Alice Beam (1763-1858), daughter of Beamsville founder Jacob Beam in 1782 and together they had a family of ten children. One son, Charles Kitchen (1799?-1870), was living in Waterloo when he met Mary Jane Nixon (1801-1847), a resident of Grimsby who was from another well-known Loyalist family. Their wedding took place in Grimsby on June 7, 1820. One sister of Charles, named Sarah or Sally, married Lewis Whitney in Grimsby in 1816. This might explain why William received the name Whitney when he was born. William was to be an only child.

At some point, William moved to Iowa where he may have met his wife, Jane. They would have six children, three boys and three girls between 1844 and 1863. Unfortunately, his mother Mary Jane died in Grimsby in 1847 when William was only 23- years-old. In the states he appears to have developed an interest in cattle, returning in 1858 to Grimsby where his father had recently purchased a large property just to the west of the town. By this time, the Great Western Railway was running through the Niagara Peninsula. There was a station in Grimsby that offered connections elsewhere, including to the United States. This village of almost 1000 people would rapidly evolve as the hub of the Niagara fruit industry. The railway proved a boon to Kitchen and others for selling their produce beyond the local market.

The next year, in 1859, Kitchen planted a large orchard and grapery. The *Illustrated Historical Atlas of the Counties of Lincoln and Welland* in 1862 and 1876 delineates the Kitchen property as Lot 12 on the western edge of Grimsby, running from the shore of Lake Ontario on the north side to a gravel road on the south side (the future Highway Eight). Here William and his sons would operate a cattle farm described as one of the "choicest herds of short-horned Dutchess Cattle in America, valued at over $100,000" (H.R. Page). Under the name The Grimsby Thoroughbred Shorthorn Stock Farm, the well-to-do Kitchen won several first-place prizes in provincial, county, and township fairs. The orchard, which he called Pleasure Grove, was located on the north half of the farm right by the lake, not far from the cattle. The farm was separated in two, almost equal parts by the railway line that ran east-west through the peninsula.

On the other side, Kitchen had his grapes, his house, and his outbuildings, including what would be the location of the winery. He became good friends with a neighbour named Jonathan Robins Pettit, who also had grapes on his farm, and the two became involved in a winery on the Kitchen farm. In 1866 an ad was placed in the *Canadian Almanac* promoting "W.W. Kitchen's Pure Grape Wine, Wholesale and Retail." This wine had taken a special prize at the Provincial Exhibition in Hamilton in 1864 and three diplomas at the last Provincial Exhibition in London. If we can believe the ad, which tells us that the wine was in use by "some hundreds of Churches for Sacramental Services" as well as being sold by "the principal chemists in Canada East and West," the wine was a huge success, perhaps due as much to its price as it quality. The wine sold for a mere $2.50 a gallon with a 25% discount for orders over ten gallons!

Kitchen also sold grapevines "at low rates by the 1000." In February, 1867, he advertised both his "pure wine and grapevines" – grape wine, Port, and Sherry, and 80,000 vines and, a year later, in the *Canada Farmer* of April 1868, Kitchen advertised choice grapevines with good roots at ten cents a vine by the 100 or the 1000! And the choice? You could buy Delawares, Concords, Dianas, Hartford Prolific, and a grape he called Oporto. However, we can safely assume that Kitchen was using most of these grapes to make his wine that now amounted to some 20,000 gallons. And his market was diversifying. He now sold wine for medicinal purposes and communion use, and his native wine was "sent everywhere to private families and hotel keepers." Winner of first-place prizes and diplomas at provincial exhibitions, the wine was, by general agreement, "invaluable for Diarrhea and Dysentery," and "not hard to take," according to Kitchen! At a time when the Temperance movement was beginning to swell, it appears there was still some justification to sample local wine—for the sake of a healthy body and soul! Such would be a prime reason for consuming Ontario wine for many years to come.

By this time, a second winery was up and running in Cooksville. This was an operation that appeared to have much more political support than the winery of Kitchen and his three sons, and yet his business continued to prosper. The 1869 *Province of Ontario Gazetteer and Directory* comments as follows: "W.W. Kitchen is extensively engaged in the manufacturing of wine, turning out about 500 barrels of a very superior article per annum. The vineyard occupies 11 acres." Kitchen had been able to access some of the better grapes that were coming available from the United States, and he had become knowledgeable in propagating them himself. Certainly, his entrepreneurial talents were sound indeed.

Kitchen was very much a realist in the work he undertook, and yet at the same time he must have had a dream of building a significant operation on his farm. Around 1868, in order to fulfill his dream, he attempted to encourage local citizens to invest in a company which was to include "Grimsby grape growing, winemaking, and a fruit canning company." As the Treasurer of Union Lodge #7 in town, Kitchen circulated a flyer to his lodge brothers promoting the sale of the company stock. There were 500 shares available at $100 each and for each share that a brother sold he would receive $5. With the way his pure grape wines were selling (we are not too sure about the rhubarb wine that he also made!) this might have been a good investment, but the company does not appear to have been incorporated.

Two years later, Kitchen tried again, hoping to raise $40,000 with 1000 shares selling at only $40 each in what our vintner described as the Grimsby Union Wine Company. His Grimsby vineyards of some ten acres of "excellent soil," all of the stock of wine estimated at 80,000 pint bottles, and all of his nursery stock were included in the offering. Kitchen also listed his winemaking assets including two large wine cellars, casks and fermenting tanks, a grape mill, a wine press, and a grape house along with a 13-room house for use by the individual who would become the Managing Director of the company. If you became a stockholder, you were promised wine and choice grapevines at the original cost of production as well as a large annual cash dividend. Unfortunately, despite the endorsement of several local ministers and doctors, the prospectus failed to entice enough people to buy up all the stock,

Nevertheless, in 1873 Kitchen sold $10,000 worth of wine and the following year $5,000 worth of fruit (grapes, apples, peaches, pears, and cherries). At that point, according to the *Illustrated Historical Atlas of 1876* he reached sales of over 50,000 gallons of native wine. Kitchen made port and sherry using Delaware grapes for the sherry, which sold for three dollars per gallon. The port, probably made from Concord and/or Oporto, was cheaper at two dollars per gallon. And, ever the entrepreneur, Kitchen continued to offer good deals with a 15% discount on ten-gallon purchases, 20% on 20 gallons, and 25% on 40 gallons.

In a marketing venture that surely was ahead of its time, Kitchen created two very picturesque coupons which he called Commission Scrip in one dollar and two dollar denominations to be used for cash purchases of over $10 and $20 dollars respectively. Both coupons show abundant grapes, barrels, and wine in bottles. On the reverse side he indicated that his prices were "lower than others who sell as good production" adding "my object in issuing this scrip is to advertise my productions, and give customers the benefit of all their money, instead of paying agents to travel and solicit orders." His grape wine was selling at two dollars per gallon, with kegs to hold it for one dollar each, and extra-fine bearing Concord vines for one dollar each. And with every purchase over ten dollars came a "receipt for making grape wine!" The canning factory, said to be the first in Canada, opened at about the same time in a drive shed on the west side of the Kitchen home.

A few years later, at the 1893 World Columbian Exposition in Chicago, Kitchen won a medal for his unfermented grape juice, a product that had become very popular due to the Temperance movement.

Sadly, on December 9th 1909, Kitchen would pass away while on a visit to Rochester, New York. He is buried in St. Andrew's Anglican Church cemetery, which is next door and on the east side of the farm that he loved so much. There are stories of discovering patches of heavily stained earth in the cemetery, which some believe indicate places where Kitchen disposed of the dregs of his winemaking or perhaps of any wine that was not suitable for sale. This may never be proven for sure, but in the efforts of William Whitney Kitchen to establish a vineyard and produce wine in Grimsby we can clearly see the beginnings of our wine industry, and there would be no turning back!

And any time you pass through Grimsby, drive along the Queen Elizabeth highway just to the west of Ontario Street, and know that you are actually driving across what was once the Kitchen farm. It is today the site of subdivisions, businesses, and the Grimsby High School, but it was long ago the site of, arguably, Ontario's first commercial winery.

Winemaking at Clair House, Cooksville:
Prejudice, politics, and a prophecy!

> Parker (Sir Henry) had managed to obtain a few tons of grapes from his own vineyard and made some champagne, and sherry and sold some of it.
>
> —Jarrell, "Justin De Courtenay and the Birth of the Ontario Wine Industry," *Ontario History*, 2011
>
> ...the last Report of the Bureau of Agriculture, proves the complete success which has attended the experiment in the cases of Mr. De Courtenay ... and Mr. Henry Parker, who lives at Cooksville near Toronto. The country ought to feel deeply indebted to both these gentlemen.
>
> —Catharine Parr Trail, *The Canadian Settlers' Guide*, 1860.

A notable feature of the Provincial Exhibition was the large quantity of wine shown in bottles, mostly produced in the neighbourhood of Hamilton, and much of it of very good quality. There are now several vineyards of considerable extent in this section, amongst which may be specially mentioned that of the Mssrs. Parker of Cooksville, which consists, as I understand, of some 50 acres, and has already gained considerable celebrity, under the able direction of Mr. De Courtenay. It seems highly probable that this new and attractive industry may, at no very distant day, become an important and profitable branch of Canadian agriculture.

—*Province of Canada, Sessional Papers*, 1866.

By the 1820s what was then known as Harrisville, an area at the crossroads of what is today Dundas Street and Huron Street, had already begun to develop as an important center of busy rural life. Jacob Cook became a leading entrepreneur in the village running the stagecoach lines to several destinations and carrying the mail from York to as far as Niagara. He had purchased 100 acres at the crossroads in 1819 for $30. There he would later build the Cooksville House Tavern. Among other endeavours, he served as the local magistrate. Considering his contributions to the village, it is no wonder that it was renamed in his honour in 1836. Today the name Cooksville is almost forgotten given that this former hub of economic life in Toronto Township has been overtaken by the sprawling City of Mississauga. However, during the 1850's and 1860's, this village of nearly 400 people become well known for its vineyard and winery activity, indeed "a rare thing in Canada" at that time.

In 1841 Sir William George Parker, a Vice-Admiral in the British Navy, left England to retire in Cooksville with his wife Elisabeth and some of their six children. The property which they bought, Lot 17 Concession 1, NDS, was in fact the very location settled originally by John Schiller. In her book *Dixie: Orchards to Industry*, Kathleen Hicks tells us that John's sons William and Michael took over his vineyard and continued his winery business for a few years, adding that "Schiller's vineyard thrived under many ownerships over the years." The reference to the sons and to the vineyard, while intriguing, cannot be substantiated, inspiring historian Richard Jarrell to label the tale "rural legend."

We do not know why Sir William decided to settle in this particular location, but the property itself would become the site of a vineyard long after Schiller's death in 1816 and would indeed change hands several times in subsequent years beginning with the Parker family. Based on Kathleen Hick's comment, some might believe that there were already grapes growing on the property, grapes that originated 30 years earlier with Schiller. However, there is simply no other reference or evidence to support this. At the same time, one might wonder why someone coming from England in the 1840s, someone most likely without any viticultural experience, would begin to plant grapes.

Some time before Sir William's death in March of 1848, work was started on a wonderful family mansion, which was given the name Clair House. It was a large and magnificent two-storey stone chateau on the north side of Dundas Street. Sons Henry (born 1822) and Melville (born 1824)—who had just recently married Maria Jane and Jessie Hector, sisters from Toronto—were left to deal with the property after their father's death. At this point, and for reasons that may never be known, the family developed an interest in growing grapes, even though grapes were still considered somewhat of a novelty here with only a few enthusiasts pursuing garden plantings. It is true that American hybrids were available from area nurseries including that of the Beadle's in St. Catharines and that of George Leslie on King St. E. in Toronto (he is known to have carried some 27 varieties of seedlings including Clinton, Catawba, Concord, Delaware, Diana, and Isabella that were all serviceable for winemaking as well as a few *vinifera* like Zinfandel, Chasselas, and a Muscat). In short, we are left wanting to know more about this very early venture in grape-growing, a venture that is, indeed, rooted in mystery!

In any case, while there is little evidence from the early 1850s, the dusty old records of Cooksville certainly speak proudly of the resulting vineyard and, in the *Canadian Directory* for 1857-58, brothers Henry and Melville Parker are listed as grape growers. After the death of his father and his elder brother Sir George (d. 1857), Henry was now Sir Henry, a Baronet, and seemed to be the driving force behind the farm. It is most probable that their grapes were native American hybrids, mainly the Clinton, and certainly not *vinifera*. In a letter dated October, 1859 from a William Hinks, Professor of Natural History at the University of Toronto, to William Hutton, Secretary of the Bureau of Agriculture in Quebec, Lower Canada, the professor refers to a letter from Henry Parker ("an intelligent man of considerable practical experience") in which Parker says that the Clinton vine is the "hardiest of all that are useful ... but that it is probable with the system of close pruning, the Catawba and the Isabella grapes ... would flourish" and that "Mr. Parker confirms my view that trying the European grapes in this climate would be useless." Hinks concludes: "I will endeavour at a suitable season, if I live, to visit Mr. Parker's vineyard."

At this point, a rather enigmatic individual enters the picture—Justin McCarthy de Courtenay, an Englishman whose name has him described by later writers erroneously as a Frenchman, Count de Courtenay. His wife, Blanche, was French and de Courtenay had worked previously in French vineyards in Perigord and in Italy. He first came to Lower Canada where his interest in growing grapes might have suggested that he was French—but a French aristocrat he was not!

From the moment he settled in the Eastern Townships of Lower Canada, near the village of Bury, probably sometimes in 1858, the 37-year-old De Courtenay zealously began to pursue his passion for grapes, planning to grow some on the property he called Val De Courtenay. On August 3, 1859 he wrote a letter to Alexander Galt, Minister of Finance for the province of Canada, in which he outlined in detail his vision to start a 10-acre vineyard with cuttings from Switzerland as the first step in a mission to convert Canadian land into vineyards. Galt passed the letter on to William Hutton who referred it to Professor Hinks and Henry Parker for their opinions. In this way, news of De Courtenay's efforts to convince the government in Lower Canada (Canada East) of the merits of growing grapes there travelled to Upper Canada (Canada West) where it initiated the correspondence that introduced De Courtenay to Henry Parker.

Writing in September, 1859, Henry Parker commented: "The resources of Canada can never be developed unless such men as Mr. de Courtenay meet with every encouragement." In 1860 the correspondence was published in the *Journals of the Legislative Assembly*, and this inspired others interested in agriculture to support the idea of growing grapes, even though they were unsure which grapes would grow well enough to allow commercial winemaking. However, De Courtenay had developed theories about the likelihood of growing grapes successfully in Canada and was lobbying politicians to secure financial support to put his beliefs to the test. Indeed, in 1863 he would publish a pamphlet entitled *The Culture of the Vine and Emigration* in which he expressed his conviction that grapes could not only grow in Lower Canada, also that they would make better wine than in Burgundy. He further declared: "there is no reason why we should not produce better ones on the borders of the St. Lawrence." He, too, was well aware of Henry Parker's efforts and commented in a letter: "As far as I can understand, Mr. Parker has cultivated only sweet water or eating grapes. If he made additions to his plants, by obtaining some, I am persuaded he would succeed as he well deserves." De Courtenay was not happy that Parker disagreed with him on the usefulness of imported vines and added. "I can discover no argument whatever in his letter demonstrating that any proper means have ever been adopted for the introduction of valuable or other European grapes." Perhaps Justin was simply not aware of the previous 250 years of failure in the United States with such grapes!

De Courtenay was also unhappy that others, like Professor Hinks, disagreed with his beliefs. In September 1859 Hinks had written to William Hutton about the efforts of Mr. De Courtenay to acquire funding to plant grapes and make wine in Lower Canada. His very sensible letter went on to say: "I have carefully considered Mr. De Courtenay's paper respecting wine culture in Canada. He evidently understands the subject practically and has referred also to good authorities ... I incline to the opinion that the true vine (*Vitis vinifera*) does not come to perfection without glass in this climate, and that our chance of successful grape culture lies in choosing good varieties derived from native species. ... It is quite possible that the hardier kinds derived from American stocks might answer and yield good wine when the European species would fail. If he can succeed in introducing wine as an additional branch of Canadian industry, I should think he would be a public benefactor and I see no impossibility of its being done with American vines." De Courtenay did admit that it might be possible to graft two varieties of Burgundy grapes that were grown in Belgium onto Clinton rootstocks—an idea that would indeed be put to the test a few years later, but in *Phylloxera*-ravaged Europe!

As it turned out, the professor's words were quite prophetic. Despite such commentary, which he considered to be negative—and although he had not received any of the financial support originally promised (Louis-Victor Sicotte, the Attorney General for Canada East and Deputy Premier had promised De Courtenay $1000)—De Courtenay went ahead in the fall of 1862 and made wine that he described as "a good sound wine." He sent some to Premier Sicotte on January 15, 1863, explaining "I have now the honour to present you with samples of wine furnished by the cultivated wild grape, and am persuaded that, making allowances for the green taste which it possesses in common with almost all new wines, you will consider it equal to ordinary Burgundy, which it resembles not only in flavour but in its qualities and colour." Knowing today what we do about wine made from wild grapes, it is no wonder that the Premier was not impressed by it. As well, a colleague, the Honourable William McDougall, a former agricultural journalist and now Commissioner of Crown Lands, declared it to be sour and added his belief that wine grapes could not be grown in Canada. De Courtenay replied in a letter to the Premier that the wine was not sour but just bitter "in consequence of containing too much tannin" —a legitimate excuse for a young red wine. De Courtenay had wanted to add French grapes "cultivated by himself in the open air" but Sicotte had requested wine made only from native vines. De Courtenay added: "my object was not to make a superior wine but to produce a wine from the native grape alone." His disappointment in dealing with the obvious prejudice he faced is understandable.

No money was forthcoming, but De Courtenay, whom Tony Aspler in his *Vintage Canada,* describes as "an aggressive evangelist in the cause of Canadian wine," continued to inspire confidence in a number of people who tasted his wines, including Lewis Drummond, a judge on the Court of the Queen's Bench, who described them as "superior to the vins ordinaires imported from France," and a W.J. Bickell, Ralph B. Johnston, Shipping Master at Quebec, and finally, Judge Charles Dewey Day, Chancellor of McGill University. As well, he had managed to stir up some interest in the Bureau of Agriculture with the result that a government committee, the Select Committee on the Cultivation of the Vine in Canada, was created in June, 1864. De Courtenay, who was now friends with Henry Parker, spoke to the Committee and gave them Parker's report that references 25 acres of

Clinton vines tended by four Italian *vignerons*, a cellar full of 1863 vintage wine, and a plan for a Royal Company of Vinegrowers. The committee, in spite of the inclusion of the pessimistic McDougall, was inspired to agree that a Canadian wine industry should be developed with government assistance.

It is not surprising that De Courtenay next appears in Cooksville. There he and Henry Parker would soon work together on a commercial enterprise. The *Province of Ontario Gazeteer* of 1869 refers to a Cooksville Vinegrowers Association that was established in 1863 with 30 cultivated acres. This was possibly the first step in setting up a joint stock company that would eventually become the Canada Vine Growers Association (CVGA). The association took over Parker's vineyard, probably in late summer 1864, holding the property in trust with De Courtenay as the trustee and manager. At this time expansion began and Henry moved out of Clair House while Melville moved to another property near the vineyard called Knoyle house after their mother Elisabeth, who had come from East Knoyle, County Wiltshire in England. De Courtenay proceeded to correspond with John A. MacDonald, Attorney General for Canada West, even inviting him to visit the vineyard and operations in Cooksville! In spite of John's attraction to alcohol there is no indication that he ever paid Justin a visit.

In a letter dated December 24, 1864 to De Courtenay, MacDonald said he would try to help with the matter and obtain "the redress which I think government owes you." De Courtenay then proceeded over the winter of 1864-1865 to produce a kind of wine that was truly a rarity in the entire wine world at the time, a local version of *eiswein*. In fact he produced both a red and a white *vin congele* as he called it, and in his pamphlet from 1866 entitled *The Canada Vine Grower* he commented. "I consider, and my friends know, I have always considered the exportation of congealed wines to Europe as the great future of both Upper and Lower Canada." Of course today *eiswein* or icewine is indeed just that, having become since the 1980s the flagship wine of the Canadian wine Industry, though no one has ever given due credit to Justin De Courtenay as the original producer.

That same year, a Reverend A. Dixon visited the operation and found barrels and equipment and cellars under construction to store up to 20,000 gallons of wine, along with plans to make dry white and red wines, champagne, and dry sherry. At a much later date, when the CVGA would be up for re-incorporation in 1926, a Toronto lawyer named Wilfrid Mactavish outlined in an affidavit the events of 1865: "a large wine plant was built, vineyards planted, and large wine vaults extending close to one quarter of a mile underground were established, which are still there." A contemporary grape grower in Port Dalhousie, W.H. Read, wrote in the March 1866 edition of the *Canada Farmer* that "the young vineyards at Cooksville, Canada, will turn off, for 1865, 50,000 gallons of native wine, and this wine has all been purchased by the Lower Canadians. This augurs well for the future, and means nothing but real success." Obviously De Courtenay had been very busy with the winery and with winemaking. More importantly, the wines were selling well. Richard Jarrell describes this as "the first commercial vineyard and winery in Canada" without commenting on the slightly earlier operations of William Kitchen in Grimsby. Still, clearly a true wine industry was at last becoming a reality!

The association took a step up the political ladder in 1866 when an Act of the Province of Canada affirmed the incorporation of the company as the Canada Vinegrowers' Association with power to issue $100,000 worth of stock at $100 a share, a large proportion of which had already been bought. Partners included Charles Day—whom Henry Parker had helped arrange the purchase of 160 acres for $20,000 in December, 1865—Ralph B. Johnston, John Hector from Toronto—who was Henry and Melville's brother-in-law—and William F. Doherty, a local farmer and prosperous land-owner. President of the group was D.W. Beadle of St. Catharines, who commented that one of the objects of the association was "to encourage farmers to cultivate the vine by affording them a market for their grapes at remunerative prices." The Act incorporating the operation exempted them from all excise duties and other imposts, except municipal or local taxes, for a period of ten years, a political gesture that aided their acquisition of investors.

Continuing to seek investment, De Courtenay attended a meeting of the Fruit Growers' Association in Grimsby in October 1866, where he offered his insights into winemaking and into the merits of grapes being grown at the time. During the meeting, he spoke about the training of the vines at Clair House, adding that the oldest part of the vineyard had produced 15 tons of grapes per acre—no mean feat then! He commented that the County of Lincoln might do even better, given that it enjoyed a more favourable climate than Cooksville. He also talked about making claret to sell for 50 cents a gallon, as well as brandy. Then he invited the group to visit Clair House. At this meeting it is likely that De Courtenay met fellow winemaker William Kitchen given that Kitchen subscribed to 50 shares in the new corporation. However, with Kitchen's own plans now developing, it seems that he never got around to paying for them, an issue that upset De Courtenay somewhat. De Courtenay continued to market his operation, speaking in February 1867 to the County of Lincoln Grape Growers' Association in St. Catharines and in October at a meeting of the Fruit Growers' Association at Clair House Vineyards itself.

Shortly afterwards, another act was passed by the new Dominion government, called the Inland Revenue Act, when it was discovered that the Association also wanted to operate a distillery, and that it intended to add sugar in the winemaking process (saccharine matter!). Obviously, the sugar added to create higher alcohol in the wine was not derived from the farm itself, and this posed a problem to some bureaucrats relating to the creation of alcohol, which they considered should allow the government to charge duty. This act, in revoking their exemption from excise duties, proved disastrous to the operations as it caused creditors to ask for their money back and almost ruined the business. D.W. Beadle, on behalf of the business, petitioned the government to repeal the offending clause and eventually it was suspended. On May 22, 1868, "to encourage the cultivation of vines and the manufacture of wine in the Dominion," the brand-new Canadian government passed an act respecting the Canada Vine Growers' Association, affirming the previous incorporation of the CVGA, and extending the grace period from excise taxes for two more years after the expiration of the ten years of the provincial Act until 1878. Everything appeared very fine indeed at this point. A Mr. John O'Connor, M.P. for Essex, moved in the House of Commons that a special committee be appointed to inquire into the desirableness and practicality of cultivating the vine and making wine in Canada, saying: "the experiments which had been recently made, more especially these which had been made on a somewhat extensive scale at Cooksville, had dispelled the prejudice which previously existed in the public mind that the climate of Canada was unsuited for cultivating the vine." Little did Mr. O'Connor know that the grapes to which he was referring would themselves fall victim to another kind of prejudice some 100 years later!

In 1866, the energetic de Courtenay, still pursuing his passion, published a second pamphlet in Toronto this time entitled *The Canadian Vinegrower: How every farmer in Canada may plant a vineyard and make his own wine*. Indeed, the CVGA advertised the sale of vine cuttings in the April 1867 *Canada Farmer* for one dollar for a hundred, along with the enticement of a free copy of the journal. Miles W. Cook, son of Jacob, who would be listed as manager of the CVGA by the 1869 *Province of Ontario Gazeteer and Directory*, planted six varieties just south of Cooksville and participated in the harvest at Clair House, which that year yielded a modest 2.5 tons per acre.

De Courtenay was soon inspired to enter some of his wines in the upcoming international Exposition in Paris, 1867 and, in spite of the challenge in sending wine overseas, managed to astonish the judges with his Canadian wine. The result was a medal, the first ever for an Ontario wine in an international competition! Two years later, in a letter to Samuel Tilley, Minister of the Customs Department that concerned bureaucratic interference with the company's purchases of imported goods, De Courtenay would be moved to declare: "I have proved by practical operation that no finer vineyard exists in Europe than the one I have created at Clair House, and have proved by receiving from the Paris Exhibition the 'only' medal accorded to American wines..." De Courtenay had every reason to be proud about his achievement, an achievement others had noted with considerable pride as attested by the July 8th, 1867 edition of *The Leader*, a Toronto newspaper:

The French exposition has established the character of our Canadian wines. The jury on wines, which would naturally be composed of the best judges to be found in Europe, speak in very high terms of the wines sent from the Clair House Vineyards, Cooksville ... They say of those wines that they resemble more the great French table wines than any other foreign wines they have examined, and that the fact of the wine being so 'solide' as to bear the sea voyage, and the variations of heat and cold without losing anything of either its quality or limpidity, should be a question of great consideration even to our own producers.

The red wine was judged to be of "excellent quality" and bearing "a resemblance to the Beaujolais wine, which is known to be the best produced in France." Supporting this evaluation was the analysis carried out by Dr. Croft, first Chemistry Professor of the University of Toronto, who declared that the red wine "had an exceedingly pleasant taste, perfectly sound and excellent, containing about 13% of alcohol." Although the Reverend Dixon commented that they were believed to be of the Douro variety, the grapes were likely Clinton, given that *The Canada Farmer* of December 15th, 1870 reported that the vineyard was "stocked with a large number of varieties, the Clinton being the leading kind in point of quantity [and were] imported by Melville Parker from Spain." This sounds like good marketing more than reality for that time, although we might recall the use of a grape called Oporto by Kitchen in Grimsby! The same Reverend Dixon also tells us that freshly-picked grapes were spread on straw to complete the maturing process and increase the sugar level by concentrating the juice. This might explain how the alcohol was able to reach 13% in grapes not known for abundant sugar; it also shows how the winemaker was able to avoid adding sugar, a step that was generally considered unacceptable at this time. Dr.Croft also found that a white wine was "sound, being free of acetic acid with a pleasant, fruity, subacid taste containing about 9% of alcohol and only a trace of sugar." However, the variety of grape is unknown.

In any case, it is clear that as a winemaker De Courtenay had made a successful beginning, even if the wines were made dry, a style that made quality difficult to achieve with the North American hybrids then available and which, apparently, was not really popular when compared to other beverages with a higher alcohol content or wines which were fortified and sweetened, wines favoured by people living in a cold climate. As well, *The Toronto Leader* commented on an even greater challenge.

This authoritative opinion of the quality of Ontario wine will do more than anything else that could possibly occur at present, to bring this wine into general use. A new kind of wine always has to make its way against settled prejudices; and in the present case, where the supposition has been general that this was not a wine-producing country, simply because we had not measured our resources, the difficulty was greatly increased. The use of the light wine by the people is increasing every year. Probably there are now a hundred gallons of claret drunk in Toronto where one was drunk ten years ago; and this implies a general cultivation of a taste for the lighter wines, which will tell upon the demand for Canadian wine.

The newspaper went on to make a tremendously prophetic statement about the benefits of making these lighter wines for a population that, from the beginning of Upper Canada, had been so enamoured of high alcohol drinks. The statement marks a defining moment in our wine history:

The time will come, we hope and verily believe, when grape-growing and wine-making will be one of the principal employments of our population. And when it does come, the cause of temperance will be advanced to a degree which could be reached by no other process.

This was all very exciting material for the brand-new country of Canada, and it makes what developed in Cooksville for De Courtenay's winery all the more a mystery. Given its charter, its freedom from excise taxes, the groundswell of political support and Melville Parker (now a Peel County Justice of the Peace), and the successful nature of the wines being produced, it is difficult to explain De Courtenay's sale of the business in 1868. Perhaps the partners had a falling out, or perhaps the business was having financial troubles—the mortgage on Clair House had never been paid and Henry Parker seems to have had little involvement in the operation. In fact, Parker sued the CVGA in 1875, stating that he had not even received interest owing. When he passed away in 1877 he had received no money at all. The undoubted reason for what happened centered around De Courtenay himself and his departure from Cooksville for Amherstburg in Essex County in the summer of 1867. A number of farmers were planning to plant grapes in that area (as well as on Pelee Island) and perhaps De Courtenay believed the potential for growing and winemaking was more favourable there. In any case, he wrote to Sir John A. Macdonald to inform him of the situation on August 22nd and indicated that he had started to grow vines on his new property. Sir John replied on October 12th, wishing him "every success." It is likely that De Courtenay had become friends with politician and lawyer John O'Connor and with his partner Solomon White, who De Courtenay seems to have interested in the operation in Cooksville. In fact, Solomon White would become the next owner of Clair House in November, 1868 with De Courtenay returning only briefly to Cooksville over the winter of 68-69, probably to help in the transition.

De Courtenay continued to correspond with the Prime Minister in 1869, apparently seeking assistance for a new enterprise; Macdonald replied that he would give the "greatest consideration." Whether this new enterprise was a winery or not is not known, but nothing came of it. De Courtenay must have been extremely disappointed. In August of 1869, Macdonald wrote to De Courtenay commenting on his decision "to desert Canada" adding that "I am not at all surprised at your having come to that conclusion as your exertions have met but scant acknowledgment." Justin De Courtenay moved back to England and leased a seven acre plot in Dorset. He would not enjoy it for long. He died in January, 1871 at only 50 years of age, having left a remarkable legacy and an encouraging example for the Ontario wine industry.

Richard Jarrell, who must be congratulated for his extensive research on De Courtenay, described him as a "visionary winemaker and advocate," and if not the industry's first winemaker, certainly its first star. Indeed, Canada's first federal Minister of Agriculture, Jean-Charles Chapais, after the Clair House success in Paris in 1867, was moved to proclaim that "Mr. De Courtenay ... may be called the father of vine culture and wine-making in Canada, if ever it becomes common here." Certainly, the achievements of Justin De Courtenay are much more solid than those of John Schiller, who has for many years been acknowledged as the 'father' of our wine Industry. Indeed, it is time to set the record straight. Justin De Courtenay believed that grape growing here was possible. In spite of the opposition from most others, and in spite of his obligation to persevere with American hybrids—which were more challenging for the production of quality wine—he managed to achieve success. Certainly, his initial efforts in Cooksville would see Clair House and the CVGA thrive for a number of years. Following his example, several others would open wineries in the decade after his departure from Canada. And it is fitting that our modern wine industry is now able to rely on *Vitis vinifera* grapes—which De Courtenay always believed would prosper here—even if we have been aided greatly by developments after his time. Should our modern wine industry ever feel the need of a founder, it should look no further than Justin de Courtenay, the man who first brought winemaking in Ontario to world prominence!

Clair House after de Courtenay: A struggle to survive

> Cooksville has—a rare thing in Canada—a vinery and wine factory under the management of Solomon White, Esq.
>
> —*Directory of the County of Peel*, 1873-4.

> There is also a vineyard in Cooksville, probably the largest vineyard in the Province, planted mainly with the Clinton, in which the fruit attains a high degree of perfection.
>
> —*The Canada Farmer 2*, 1870

The next owner of Clair House was an individual whose life story is simply fascinating, but who now remains but a name in history books. Solomon White (1836-1911) was born on the Huron reserve near Windsor. He was the son of Joseph White, Chief of the Wyandot Peoples, and a French-speaking mother. In 1865 he began to practice law at Windsor and married Mary L. Drew two years later. In 1868 he moved to Cooksville and in November purchased Clair House Vineyards and the winery.

Almost immediately the business was beset with difficulty, given that the government sought to assess duty on purchases of imported goods such as "fresh and dry grapes and other saccharine matters, Barbadoes and Jamaica spirit, and bottles and corks" according to De Courtenay. Although he had left the business, he continued to write letters to the Governor General, to Minister Tilley of Customs, and to Macdonald on behalf of Clair House seeking understanding for various operations of the business. Four years later, in March 1873, Judge Day, one of the original partners in the CVGA, wrote to the government again when Inland Revenue continued to challenge their business model, pointing out that similar government action had put the company in serious distress back in 1867. Still, winemaking continued on, according to a report of the Fruit Growers' Association of Ontario in 1873 that referred to the Cooksville vineyard as possibly "the largest vineyard in Canada (about 40 acres) ... stocked with a larger number of varieties." Three years later there were at least four other wineries operating along with Clair House in Ontario. All of them sent samples of their wine to the 1876 American Centennial Exhibition in Philadelphia. All six CVGA wines were awarded silver medals! This success was from an operation that was, according to various writers, producing approximately 50,000 gallons, and averaging about 10 tons per acre and employed at least 20 people. And the government, through an Order-in-Council in 1873, was allowing Clair House to continue to make a significant amount of brandy, one gallon for every three of wine, for a period of five years. To maintain this, White sought additional shareholders as early as 1873. The *Directory of the County of Peel, 1873-4* provides the names of several men who were by then associated with the vineyard including: Solomon White as proprietor; a Peter White (perhaps a relative); John Lamb; Thomas Cramp; three Torrance brothers, David, John, and George; and a M.G. Glassbrook. Thomas Cramp had, by 1870, become managing partner in the Montreal firm of David Torrance and Company, a wholesale and retail grocery company trading largely in tea, wines, and liquors. That year, the firm created a Toronto branch called Cramp, Torrances and Company, an importer of coffee, tea, and sugar, that was located on Front Street. This company quickly prospered doing sales of $1 million in 1872. Such businessmen would prove a valuable asset to Solomon, who ran (unsuccessfully) for a seat in the Provincial Assembly for Peel County in 1873.

The operation appears to have been "a prosperous grape and wine business," according to the *Dictionary of Canadian Biography*. Even so, in 1876, shortly before the approaching deadline on excise taxes, Solomon decided to sell Clair House after some eight years as proprietor. He then returned to the Windsor area where he operated a farm with grapes, cattle, and horses. He also resumed his law practice. He served in Provincial Government both in 1878-1886 and in 1890-1894 when, as the first aboriginal legislator in Ontario, he became the first to voice native concerns, defending various native land claims. He lost popularity with his own party, however, when he sought the annexation of Ontario to the United States, as well as the implementation of French as the sole language in French schools. To top off this most unusual career, he was acting Mayor of Cobalt in Northern Ontario when he died in 1911.

The *Walker and Miles Atlas of Peel County* of 1877 clearly shows the location of the Canada Vinegrowers Association property. It was almost cut in half by the Credit Valley Railway, which is just to the west of what is now Hurontario Street. It straddled both sides of Dundas Street. Close by was the property that was still owned by Melville Parker. *The Canadian Journal of Medical Science*, makes a lengthy comment on the winery, telling us that the well-known firm of Cramp, Torrance, and Co:

have become proprietors of the business of the CVGA. This Association has recently been re-organized, and according to the reports of experienced analysts such as Professor Croft of Toronto University and Professor Ellis of

Introducing grapes to Upper Canada and Ontario: 1790-1880

the School of Practical Science, manufactures wines and brandies, perfectly pure, as far as chemical tests can prove them so.

With the help of the Toronto wholesalers, who had offices in Toronto and Montreal, the wines of Clair House continued to reach a wide audience. Mr. James White, the representative of the Company, travelled across Canada to promote the wines by showing commendatory letters from several Toronto physicians. Samples of the wines—now seemingly sweeter in style, included Sauterne, Savigny, Vin de Porto, and Madeira, that were made from grapes on the then 70 acres, and that were at least four years old—were exhibited at the meeting of the Canada Medical Association in Hamilton, and were highly approved of by many of those present. Mention is made of the medals awarded in Paris in 1867, as well as those from the Centennial Exposition at Philadelphia in 1876. An interesting ad in *The Canada Medical Record* of January of 1878, tells us that Messrs McGibbon and Baird of Montreal keep the wines of the CVGA for sale, either in wood or bottle! And the comment was made that "for patients requiring mildly stimulating wines, these appear to be well adapted." But by this time, there was competition from a number of new wineries in Niagara, Toronto, and on Pelee Island, and the winery would begin a slow decline until, in 1926, its original charter expired.

A succession of owners followed, along with the changes in the business. George Torrance appears to have had some success for a while. A reference in the Credit Valley Railroad records of 1882 adds that the winery "produces 50,000 gallons of wine per year," maintaining the production of earlier years. In 1887 Torrance sold it to Benjamin Murray, who in turn sold it to Andrew Aikens in 1891. Andrew had only five men employed in the vineyards, but he continued to produce wine until 1903 when he sold the operation to a French immigrant named Achilles Roumegous. Roumegous and his son continued to operate a smaller-scale vineyard and rabbit farm on the property until Achilles died in 1926. This was at the same time that the CVGA appears to have stopped producing wine and became defunct.

The story has an unhappy ending. On March 18th 1932 Clair House was razed by fire and destroyed. The property was sold to Ernest Webb, who demolished the remains of the vineyard in 1935 to make way for new construction. Apparently as late as 1950 you could still see remnants of the "caves" along with a few gnarled old vines. One of the few reminders of Clair House is the name of a laneway that once led to the old estate. This laneway is now called Parkerhill Road in reference to the original owners— the Parker family.

The Parkers, who started it all, De Courtenay, who in a few short years took a fledgling wine industry to new heights, the Clinton grape, and even the town of Cooksville itself, have become virtually forgotten names in what today constitutes our modern grape and wine industries. Yet, an argument could be made that Clair House was Canada's first commercial winery, with a vineyard established shortly before Kitchen's vineyard in Grimsby and with grapes growing and wines sold several years before what would become Ontario's third wine operation, Vin Villa on Pelee Island, that often receives undue credit as Ontario's first winery.

Pelee Island: A pure, native wine industry on Canada's island in the sun

> Two winery structures from the last century are prominent and remain in good repair. These are presently used as homes, as in the last century when they belonged to the Wardroper and Rehberg families. Two other edifices—the Vin Villa Winery and the Finlay Winery--are in ruin, partly hidden by local flora ... A fifth winery, the Wine House owned by J.S. Hamilton of Brantford, has left its mark on the local topography. A visible knoll remains as evidence ... A sixth winery, for which no site evidence is available, likely belonged to Charles Heaton.
>
> —Tiessen *The Vinedressers*, 1997.
>
> I find that the public generally prefers native wines after they have begun to use them.
>
> —Haskins, *Ontario Agricultural Commission Report*, 1880.
>
> A major factor in the location of the grape industry on Pelee Island and its subsequent spread to the mainland was the

influence of the nearby American islands on which grapes grew well.

—Weber, *A History of the Vineyard and Wine Industry of Essex County*,1971.

For many people, Pelee Island has long been a special place, given that it is the most southerly point in all of Canada. This island of some 10,000 acres, an entire township in the County of Essex, is located in Lake Erie about 100 km south-east of Windsor and only 22 miles from Sandusky Ohio, which is on the Canada-US border. Only nine miles long and three to four miles in width, it offers a climate that can be mild in winter with early springs and warm summers leading into an autumn of extended frost-free days—a wonderful environment for grapevines. On Kelley's Island, just 12 miles south of Pelee, North American hybrid grapes had taken root as early as 1842 with plantings of both Catawba and Isabella. Soon, the same vines would make their way to Pelee. The American islands to the south quickly created a successful grape growing industry along with a number of wineries, and it was only logical that someone would see a similar potential on Pelee.

In his well-researched book on *The History of Grape Farming and Wineries on Pelee*, Ron Thiessen remarks: "It is thought the year was 1854 when the first grapevines were planted on Pelee Island by Henry Price." Price was an American from Cleveland. Although Price's vineyard was small and unsuccessful, Pelee would prove to be a welcome home for the late-ripening but highly-desired Catawba grape when just a dozen years later the first significant attempts at vineyard development would be made by other newcomers to the island, men from the United States who had sights on both grape growing and winemaking.

The American Civil War brought many changes to the lives of all Americans, especially those who sided with the South. One man in particular—a grape grower and winemaker and rebel sympathizer—decided to leave his home in Kentucky and move his family to Canada. In Windsor, D.J. Williams met Captain David McCormick, whose father was head of the original family of settlers on Pelee, and went touring with the Captain around the Lake Erie Islands. In August of 1865 he returned with his brother Thomas and a relative named Thaddeus Smith, also from Kentucky. They bought a 40 acre property at the north end of the island for $4000 and formed a partnership: Smith, Williams and Co. Wasting no time, the next year they planted 25 acres of grapes and would add eight more over the next three years. They proceeded to excavate a wine cellar 40' x 60' and built the winery and a house above, an attractive two-and-a-half storey building they called Vin Villa which they completed by 1868.

Thaddeus Smith spent the summer of 1867 working on the property, then moved his wife Adelia and two daughters Bertha and Minnie Bird into the house when it was ready. Pelee itself was developing into a busy and well-knit community with about 150 residents, one church, two schoolhouses, and its first store, all by 1870. Regular steamboat service would be forthcoming. Thaddeus by this time had already proven his ability as a grape grower and reported yields of four to five tons per acre of Catawba, Delaware, and other varieties that were now growing in the Vin Villa vineyard.

In the autumn of 1865, D.J. Williams invited two fellow Englishmen to visit Pelee Island, These men were both rebel sympathizers living in Alabama whom he had met in Kentucky. The two brothers, Edward and John Wardroper, must have liked what they saw as the following year they purchased 15 acres of land on the west side of the island. Other islanders were also now planting grapes, so that by 1869 there were over 60 acres of American hybrids. Williams and Smith's were the largest at 33 acres, followed by the Wardroper's with nine, and several members of the McCormick clan had plots ranging from two to six acres. Numerous other individuals would follow their example resulting in some 40 vineyards and a surge of plantings, adding up to some 225 acres over the next 20 years.

In addition to Vin Villa and the winery of the Wardropers, growers Charles Heaton, James Srigley, John Finlay, and Henry Rehberg, who all arrived in the late 1800s, would also create wineries. The origins of these men were diverse. They came from Germany, Ireland, and from other locations in Ontario, and would add an interesting mix to the industry. This was truly an exciting era on Pelee and, with the first sale of wines coming in the early 1870's, Ontario had its third wine region following Niagara and Cooksville.

In keeping with the developing interest in grapes—grapes represented the third most significant fruit crop in Ontario by the 1870's— the Pelee Island growers would plant an ever-increasing variety, both for winemaking purposes and for market use. Although somewhat prone to mildew, the Catawba dominated from the beginning here, and made Pelee the prime growing region for Catawba in Ontario. Others that were planted on the island included the Concord and the Delaware, both highly favoured, as well as the Isabella, Clinton, Hartford Prolific, Ives, Iona, Roger's, Norton's Virginia Seedling, and Niagara. Charles Heaton developed a hybrid of his own by crossing Catawba with Concord and grew the grape on his property, naming it Island Queen. All in all, this was an impressive line-up of the best and most popular American hybrids available in the province, and with this line-up would come booming employment and business for the islanders, along with considerable development for the island.

Of all the wineries that would evolve on Pelee, the first to plant and start production, Vin Villa Vineyards, was largely responsible for the winemaking success that was to follow. Several photos of the winery and its excavated double-vaulted cellar and its equipment, reveal the seriousness of an operation that eventually became the responsibility of Thaddeus Smith. In 1871, a man named John Schulthies, originally from Germany but then living in Kentucky, was brought in to manage the vineyard. He arrived with his wife and four children for the first vintage and took up residence in a house built for them near Vin Villa. At least part of the first crop was exported to Sandusky, and it is possible some wine was made at this time. In 1873, Thaddeus became sole owner of the business. Wine was already being made on site and, despite what could be considered today rather rustic fermenting conditions, it appears that the wine was of very acceptable quality.

At this time Ontario wine was certainly not in great demand given that it had only been available for about a decade, and that no real market had yet been developed for it. But Thaddeus had plenty of wine to sell and, after having no luck at all on the nearby mainland with a hired salesman, he himself went on the road to sell his wine. An encounter with a young businessman in Brantford, Joshua S. Hamilton, who had started a grocery/liquor business there in 1871 would prove fortuitous, not only for Thaddeus and for Pelee Island but also for the nascent Ontario wine industry. The two men, despite the difference in their ages, hit it off very well and Hamilton agreed to take all the wine for the business, now named Hamilton, Dunlop, and Co., becoming the sole agent for Vin Villa wines.

By 1876 Hamilton was beginning to market and advertise the wines then available. A Dry and a Sweet Catawba at $1.20 a gallon were the first offerings of a portfolio that would soon increase dramatically. When Dunlop retired in 1877, Hamilton changed the name of the business to J.S. Hamilton and Company, planning to market the grape and wine production of Vin Villa both locally and elsewhere. The following year he took all of the remaining wine from Thaddeus to his warehouse in Brantford. Sales continued to increase and in 1881 5 casks of wine were shipped to British Columbia, the first shipment of Ontario wine to that province.

Displaying his talent as a marketer, Hamilton exhibited his wines in a variety of competitions and exhibitions, receiving considerable applause along the way. The Canadian Commissioner in London, Mr. S.F. May, commented on an exhibition of Pelee Island wines in 1878 in Paris, France, with these words: "I have much pleasure in informing you that a bronze medal has been awarded to your firm; also that His Royal Highness the Prince of Wales tasted your wines and expressed himself much pleased with the flavour and quality." Between 1879 and 1882, as detailed in the 'Amherstburg Echo' of October, 1882, Pelee branded wines garnered more prizes and an additional seven medals!

By the late 1880's, the company was acting as agent for several vineyards and other island wineries (the Wardroper wine cellar was added to their house in 1882, and in 1888 John Finlay constructed a house over his wine cellar). Between Pelee and Brantford there would be storage capacity for 250,000 gallons of several wines, "none sold less than two years old," including older vintages. By now, Hamilton was marketing his wines in several Canadian provinces, the eastern United States, the West Indies, and in Great Britain. The portfolio now featured Dry and Sweet Catawba, a claret and a dry red, a port and a sherry, and "the perfect Communion wine" named St. Augustine, a very popular and widely endorsed sweet red sacramental wine made from Concord and Catawba (the staunch Anglican Hamilton also provided an unfermented grape juice for churches requiring a non-alcoholic product!). There were varietals as well including an Isabella and a Delaware, and they all sold for $1.50 a gallon in five gallon lots or for $1.25 in barrel lots.

To help handle the increasing yield of the Pelee Island vineyards, Hamilton purchased a five acre plot on the island in 1889 with plans to build his own wine cellar. This turned out to be a three-storey, 100 x 50 foot stone building called The Wine House with the press on the third floor and several 1000 gallon vats on the lowest level. Completed in time for the harvest of 1891, the winery pressed some 50,000 gallons of wine (which was considered about one-half of the island's production) from an abundance of grapes that sold for a penny and a half a pound (Concord) up to three cents (Catawba and Delaware).

The following year Hamilton began the production of brandy, which he called somewhat controversially 'Cognac', and in 1894 he brought in equipment from Epernay, France as well as a French winemaker to produce what is possibly the first commercial Ontario "Champagne," a *Methode Champenoise* product called L'Empereur Champagne, which was released in 1898 in two formats: sec, and extra dry.

Ironically, at a time when it would have been more than appropriate to toast the success of Hamilton's investments and efforts, the future of grape growing and winemaking in Essex County would start to cloud over. In 1896, as the century came to a close, Edward Wardroper sold his wine casks to the Pelee Oil and Gas Company and prepared to leave the island. Henry Rehberg had moved to the mainland. And the pioneers of Pelee were beginning to pass on (Smith in 1902, John Wardroper in 1901 and Edward Senior in 1908) leaving something of a void. At the same time, the vines on the island were being uprooted to accommodate a much better paying crop—tobacco. Grapes had provided a decent income for many years despite some inconsistent vintages; however, after 1897, when protective duties were imposed on imported tobacco, prices began to soar for homegrown tobacco along with the price of land, and vineyards were put in jeopardy. That year in Essex County, according to the Ontario Bureau of Industries, there were almost 1100 acres of grapes, and wineries were still buying Pelee Island grapes. But tobacco acreages only continued to climb, replacing vineyards that could not compete with this new market. From a peak at 1794 in 1904 grape acres would fall to 654 only six years later and decline to 275 acres by the beginning of World War I and to less than 50 acres during the 1920s.

The removal of considerable grape acreage all over Essex County would soon take a toll on winemaking there resulting in a dramatic decline in the number of wine cellars. It would also take a toll on the Wine House, and obligate Hamilton to cease processing on Pelee with the 1914 vintage being his last. He then moved his winemaking operations to Dalhousie Street in Brantford, taking his wine to his warehouse there in 1915 before selling off many of his large casks and the Wine House itself in 1916. And so, a remarkably quiet end came to the Pelee Island saga after 50 years of significant and amazing achievement.

In 1918 the Pelee Island Wine and Vineyards Company amalgamated with the J.S. Hamilton Co. with Captain Hamilton as President and Managing Director, remaining in business through Prohibition and afterwards (in spite of his death in 1931) until 1945 when the London Winery Ltd. acquired the company.

The Wine House, which became the A.M. McCormick General Store in 1916, unfortunately was destroyed by fire in November, 1935. Vin Villa, where the grape and wine story of Pelee began, would see several changes of ownership over the years with some grapes being maintained until the 1940s. In 1950 it was abandoned, then neglected, left to become a victim to a destructive fire in 1963.

North American hybrid vines: Friend or foe?

> Phylloxera is more than a pest. It's a slow-moving monster with an insatiable appetite ... Phylloxera has been the grim reaper of modern viticulture. Being native to eastern North America, Phylloxera found European grapevines an easy target because they lacked the resistance that native American vines had developed.
>
> —Laube, Wine Spectator, 2017

> Within a quarter of a century the vineyards of France...and finally some four-fifths of the vineyards of the world, were to feel like Pharaoh at odds with Moses and his god – oidium was the first plague ... after it came phylloxera, and after phylloxera mildew ... Nothing was to be the same again after the long struggle to protect and re-establish wine-growing in Europe.

Introducing grapes to Upper Canada and Ontario: 1790-1880

—Johnson, Story of Wine, 1989

The emergence of grape growing and a native wine industry in the north-eastern American States and in Ontario depended entirely on the availability of vines that were unique to this region, the interspecific hybrids created by chance or subsequently by human effort. Because of their American wild grape parentage they proved to be very winter-hardy in places where people assumed it would be too cold for them to survive. As well, many of them were blessed with natural defenses against native grapevine diseases and pests which had proven fatal to European *vinifera* vines, and while they were not completely invulnerable to problems, this natural resistance encouraged the planting of hybrids where efforts to grow imported *vinifera* varieties had previously failed. The hybrids also tended to produce abundant crops, and that made all the work involved in planting and maintaining vineyards worthwhile. And the grapes were intriguing in themselves, making wines with a character quite different from the *vinifera* varieties with which people were familiar.

For these reasons, and because they were still somewhat of an agricultural novelty, there developed considerable interest in North American vines not only locally but also in other viticultural regions. This interest would evolve into requests to have some of the vines exported, an ordinary activity that would turn out to be the innocent beginning of what developed into an extraordinary catastrophe in Europe in just a few years.

Around 1840, shortly before the Concord grape developed as a game-changer for the North American grape and wine industries, other American hybrids had already been introduced to France for experimental wine-making purposes. However, accustomed to their own distinguished *vinifera* wines, most French oenophiles were not impressed with the foxy *labrusca* flavour and aromas of the hybrids and chauvinistically described the wines as resulting from inferior grapes. If the importations had stopped at this point, shortly before mid-century, it is likely that North American hybrids would have remained a purely local phenomena on this side of the Atlantic and the future of *vinifera* on the other side and elsewhere in the world would never have been assailed. But for grape history that was not to be the case.

By the 1850's, with steamships now crossing the Atlantic in less than two weeks, additional hybrid vines were able to be imported to Europe for horticultural experiments or botanic uses, imports that, without anyone realizing it at that time, brought along with them a trio of invisible invaders: oidium or powdery mildew, downy mildew, and finally a microscopic mite that later would come to be named *Phylloxera vastatrix*. All three were able to survive the shorter ocean crossing. Arriving in an environment where they had previously been unknown and without anyone being aware of them at first, these invaders that were borne on vines that ironically had been created in part from European *vinifera*, would quickly wreak havoc on vulnerable *vinifera* vineyards and forever change the future of winemaking. Over the next quarter century they would cause the near collapse of European winemaking and spread eventually world-wide, leaving only a few isolated pockets of *vinifera* grape-growing inviolate; in Ontario at the same time, our native grape industry—which had no *vinifera* vines to prove worrisome—was expanding almost beyond expectations.

What followed was a monumental struggle to deal with the *Phylloxera* damage that continued to spread further afield, working its way everywhere *vinifera* grapes were being grown. The entire world of grapes and wine was thrown into turmoil. As Hugh Johnson described it in *The Story of Wine*, "a total revolution brought about by one deadly pest and two recurring diseases all arriving within less than 30 years, and in some places almost simultaneously." This revolution motivated responses to protect and save the industry with consequences that would alter fundamentally the nature of grape growing everywhere including North America and … Ontario.

Carrying grapevine diseases and *Phylloxera* wherever they went, North American hybrids would prove deadly to vineyards outside our region at the same time when they were themselves the source of our own viticultural success and would continue to be so for another 100 years. It is surely one of the great ironies of history that the destruction which they brought elsewhere unwittingly would be responsible for their own demise in their own backyard a century later when they fell victim to a rather quiet 'invasion' of imported *vinifera* vines, the same species they had helped almost eradicate on earth!

The problems actually began in the early 1850's when a fungus fatal to *vinifera* vines, oidium or powdery mildew, arrived in England on specimens of American vines collected by avid botanists. It then made its way to France. This mildew spread quickly in a vineyard, weakening vines and dramatically reducing the crop. Fortunately, science was able to deliver a means of control in only a decade with the use of powdered sulphur dusted on the vines. But more significant signs of trouble began to appear in Southern France shortly after a shipment of American vines arrived there in the early 1860's. The leaves on a vine would weaken and drop off, shoots would wither, and the fruit refuse to ripen. The vines themselves began to die within three years. To make matters worse the problem spread like a plague with damage being noticed in other wine regions by 1867.

In 1868 a group of scientists including Professor Planchon of Montpellier University, and a Montpellier stock broker and vineyard owner named Gaston Bazille, closely examined a vineyard near Arles and discovered the root of the problem—a microscopic, yellowish-coloured aphid living en masse on the roots of the vines. This tiny insect fed on the tender vine roots, injecting a substance that caused small swellings or galls on them and, as it would be discovered later, caused the roots to shut down in defence, leaving the vine literally rootless. Planchon, an entomologist, named it after a similar insect that left galls on oak leaves, *Phylloxera*, adding the descriptor *vastatrix*, from the Latin meaning "the destroyer," as it appeared to consume the vine roots entirely.

A scientist named Gaston Fouex came to the conclusion that *Phylloxera* could not be of European origin or the problem would have arisen before. It must have come from a place where grapevines had developed some resistance to the insect, allowing both to survive. After visits to vineyards in America, Planchon discovered that *Phylloxera* was in fact native there and that some American vines were either partially or completely resistant. At last it was clear why importing European *vinifera* vines to America had never been successful—they had no resistance to native American grape diseases and this pest whose existence had not been noticed before. It was also clear that vines from America were the source of all the problems! Now the question became one of dealing with an insect that reproduced in incredible numbers and that passed through a stage that allowed it to fly from place to place.

As early as 1869 there was a move to graft *vinifera* vines on resistant American rootstock and re-establish French vineyards, but many believed this was a potential Pandora's box, and feared a negative impact on wine quality. Nevertheless, the search began to find *Phylloxera*-resistant rootstocks from America. At the same time, American species other than the undervalued *Vitis labrusca* (including *riparia, rupestris,* and *berlandieri*) were brought over for experimental use in grafting with *vinifera* varieties. Others preferred to try chemicals and other ingenious means including burying toads at each vine or flooding or fumigating a vineyard or having schoolboys urinate on vines in a desperate effort to eliminate the mite. Most of these had little impact beyond a temporary control and no actual 'cure' has ever been found for *Phylloxera* despite all attempts to eradicate the problem. In the end, grafting would win out as the best means of saving the vines, although at tremendous cost and effort considering the millions of vines to be considered.

Sadly, the American vines, imported in huge volumes to save the European grape industry, introduced a third misery: downy mildew, a fungus that acted to defoliate the vines. Fortunately, a French viticulturalist named Millardet found a remedy for this rather quickly, a mixture of copper sulphate and lime in liquid form that came to be called the Bordeaux mixture. Thus was created the second of two essential tools in combatting grape diseases that would allow grape-growers world-wide a means to help control both downy and powdery mildew—a significant development for helping to grow *vinifera* vines successfully in America in the twentieth century after so many previous attempts over hundreds of year had ended in failure.

The nature of the times—with ruined vintages, fraudulent wine production increasing dramatically, and the growing concern that the nature of wine and its quality would be changed forever—contributed to a burgeoning interest in the science of grape-growing and winemaking. Heading into the twentieth century, educational facilities developed in many places, at Bordeaux, Wadenswill, and Geisenheim, that provided (and continue to provide) remarkable learning for these industries.

In France a small number of individuals believed there was another way of dealing with the *Phylloxera* issue through the creation of completely new hybrid vines, crosses of non-labrusca American species with the classic European *vinifera*. Their intent was to capture the hardiness and resistance of the former with the wonderful wine quality of the latter, *sans le renard*! The result would be vines that would be less expensive to plant than grafting, and that would grow in a wider range of climatic conditions. The work of Albert Seibel (1844-1936), Francois Baco (1865-1947), Eugene Kuhlmann

(1858-1932), Bertille Seyve (1864-1939), Seyve-Villard (1895-1959), and several others, was impressive. A number of valuable hybrids resulted from the thousands created, and these would be widely planted – almost 1,000,000 acres by 1958 in France alone!

Originally known only by the hybridizer's name and a number (e.g. Seibel 9549), today many of these grapes have been given names which consumers have come to recognize like Baco Noir, Marechal Foch, De Chaunac, Seyval Blanc, and Vidal. Unfortunately, not everyone has been pleased with their wine quality especially in France itself where the vines came to be considered as "bastards," that is, poor substitutes for their cherished *vinifera*. Today they are no longer allowed to be used in French table wine production. This also explains why the French preferred to call these vines American "hybrids" while in North America they are normally referred to as "French hybrids" or "French-American hybrids."

Early in the twentieth century, the first of these new vines found their way to North America, to California—where it was hoped they might help solve the *Phylloxera* problem—and then to New York State to the Geneva Research Station, and into the hands of a few interested individuals. Just as Prohibition was coming to an end, in Ontario the first French hybrid, Seibel 1000, now called Rosette, was introduced here to local scientists from a shipment of 20 hybrids that came to Geneva on March 1, 1927 from a half dozen French hybridizers. After Prohibition ended in the United States more hybrids arrived there from France destined for a number of private individuals and their work led to the first commercial American plantings of grapes like Seibel 7053 (Chancellor) and Baco Noir (Baco #1). From this incredibly modest and quiet beginning, with only a very small group of people in the industry and at the Research Stations having any awareness of these grapes, no one would have been able to envision the revolutionary changes that were in store for Ontario winemaking.

The 1870s: More new wineries put down roots in the new province

> From an inspection of the Tillsonburg vintages we do not doubt that Canada and this portion of Ontario in particular, will be creditably represented by the above firm (S. Joy and Co.)
>
> —*The Brantford Expositor.*

> I have a vineyard near Hamilton of about 13 acres; or rather I have it in partnership with Mr. Bauer...The Clinton grows very freely, and is very prolific; the most so of any wine grape we have, and that is all we use it for. Last year (1879) we had about 28 tons of Clinton grapes and they ripened perfectly ... It makes excellent wine.
>
> —Haskins, *Ontario Agricultural Commission Report*, 1880.

> I can grow between 4 and 5 tons to the acre. From 4 tons of Concord grapes we can produce between 500 and 600 gallons of wine. I am manufacturing wine both for my own use and for commercial purposes. The value of this wine is about $1 per gallon. I consider that grape culture in our part of Essex (Sandwich) is a perfect success.
>
> —Girardot, *Ontario Agricultural Commission Report*, 1880.

> The young Thomas G. Bright, a wealthy lumberman, started the business (in Toronto) with his partner F.A. Shirriff. They called it the Niagara Falls Wine Company and sixteen years later they moved to the outskirts of that town to be near their grape supply.
>
> —Aspler, *Vintage Canada*, 1983.

Continuing through the 1870's, avid grape enthusiasts all around the new province were experimenting with an extensive and ever-lengthening list of grape varieties in their attempts to find grapes that would best suit their local conditions for winemaking. And in 1868 at least one exhibition, the Provincial Exhibition in Toronto, had divided their wine competition into both amateur and professional categories to accommodate all levels of winemaking. Building on the growing and widespread interest in grapes, other passionate entrepreneurs opened wineries to complement those in Grimsby, Cooksville, and on Pelee Island, confirming the birth of our winemaking industry.

One of the first of these, a winery opened by Dr. Sylvanus Joy of Tillsonburg, would start with the best of intentions, only to become defunct in short order. Sylvanus Joy was born in Utica, New York, on July 4, 1833 and studied there to become a doctor. As a young man he decided to move to Canada and continued his education at Queen's College in Kingston, graduating after two years in 1856. Eventually he moved to Tillsonburg and married a local girl with whom he had two daughters. Over time he served as coroner of Oxford County and was a highly respected surgeon with his own practice.

According to *The Tillsonburg News* he planted 20 acres of grapes in 1865, which he cultivated for over ten years and had "the largest apple orchard and general fruit farm in Ontario about 3 miles from Tillsonburg." Here he erected extensive vaults and produced annually 10,000 gallons of wine. Some of this was sent to the World's Fair in Paris, France and was awarded a diploma for excellence of quality. The writer of the article, Laurel Beechey, added that the wine "has become familiar and favorably known throughout the province of Ontario." The accuracy of this statement is now very difficult to ascertain, even though the reference in *The Brantford Expositor* at that time would appear to support the claim. Little else is known about the winery or its wines, although Dr. Joy himself appears to have been very active in his community. He died a wealthy man in October, 1919, and was laid to rest in a massive granite crypt in the Tillsonburg Cemetery.

In Prince Edward County, north and east of Toronto along Lake Ontario, it appears that a number of individuals had been making their own wine and some of this had been entered into competitions at various fairs. One family, that of J.H. Morden and sons of Rednersville, were making wine from their own grapes which they advertised with considerable pride in a magazine that appeared in Picton on December 14, 1865, the "North

American Newspaper." The ad declared that their wine was "superior for medicinal purposes, especially invalids, to the adulterated and drugged mixtures daily exposed for sale," a statement which reveals the lax legal attitude to the sale of homemade alcohol at the time. The ad also stated "we call the attention of church authorities to it as being highly recommended by the best judges in Canada (Canada West) and suitable for sacramental purposes." Unfortunately, we do not know what grapes were being used to make this wine, nor how long the Mordens were in business, but it seems appropriate to describe this operation as "commercial." Another man from "the County," Dorland Noxon, who was possibly a relative of the Mordens, planted vines in Hillier Township near Sophiasburgh, eight miles north-west of Bloomfield. In 1876 he submitted a wine to the Philadelphia Exposition—what can be considered the first official World's Fair, held to celebrate the 100th anniversary of the signing of the Declaration of Independence—and won a gold medal for this. Again, there is no record of the kind of grapes he used. When Prince Edward County went 'dry' in the following decades, such artisanal winemaking seems to have come to an end here and a full century would pass before there would be a resurgence of grape growing and wine making in "the County" starting in the 1990s.

A winery started in St. Catharines in 1873 would outlive all of the earlier operations, remaining in business for well over 100 years as "Canada's oldest continuously operating winery." George Barnes (born on March 8, 1812), son of a prominent lawyer in Ireland, had emigrated to Canada with his brother William in 1833, settling in Hamilton, Ontario. Eventually he would own extensive properties here, including a large area that was bounded by Sherman Avenue on the west, and Gage Avenue on the east, and that was situated between Main and King Streets where Barnesdale Avenue can still be found. Later he would establish vineyards where Vineland Avenue is located in the east end of the city.

During this latter endeavour he, in all likelihood, became acquainted with William Haskins (born May 7, 1828), also an Irishman, who had emigrated to Canada in 1852 to work for the Great Western Railroad, and who was appointed City Engineer for Hamilton in 1856. Haskins had established a 13-acre vineyard just outside the eastern edge of Hamilton in 1858 or 1859 and was keenly interested in growing grapes and making wine, as his comments to the Ontario Agricultural Commission in 1880 indicate. Haskins and his partner Henry Bauer grew several varieties of grapes including Concord, many Roger's varieties, Hartford Prolific, Delaware, Iona, Diana, Isabella, Crevelling, and others, and was proficient at rooting his own cuttings, which he did in the 1000s. His fermenting tanks held two tons of grapes, and he described in detail in the "Report" exactly how he made his wines, commenting that his ports and sherries were 'lighter' than imports but his clarets and sauternes were higher in alcohol than imported versions. He mentioned that he had a cellar where the day's picked grapes would go directly for crushing in the evening. His final words to the three-member panel of the Commission are significant: "There is a good deal of wine made in our district."

The *Illustrated Historical Atlas of the County of Wentworth* of 1875 noted that Haskins was a partner of George Barnes in a retail wine business, and that the American writer Walt Whitman is said to have visited their cellars while he was in Hamilton, but nothing else is known of this. A building in Hamilton, believed to have been built about 1903 at 33 Sanford Street, belonged to a Gerald M. Haskins of the Haskins Wine Co. with Raymond Haskins as the winemaker. It would appear that these were his sons who were carrying on the business there.

Around 1845, George Barnes opened what proved to be a successful book and office supply store called George Barnes & Co., one of the first bookstores in Ontario. But after he developed an interest in grapes, (he is said to have had family connections to grape growers in Niagara), he sold his bookstore in 1869 to Robert Duncan and John Stuart. Four years later, along with Duncan and six other men, Andrew and James Skinner, John Reid, Charles Murray, George Magan, and Thomas Barnes, the son of his brother William, Barnes applied for a charter to operate a commercial winery in St. Catharines, and received it on June 9th, 1873. The winery took the impressive title The Ontario Grape Growing and Wine Manufacturing Company Limited with access to Barnes' grapes from Hamilton and with 52 acres of grapes near the winery in an area that came to be called Barnesdale.

With its excellent location on the west side of the Welland Canal, not far from where the Queen Elizabeth Highway and Ontario Street are today, the winery prospered. The story is often told how Barnes would host various ship's captains waiting while their ship was towed through the Canal, a time-consuming process. The captains would return happily to their ships with a sampling of Barnes' products to grace their dinner table. Within 20 years, annual wine production of several varieties would reach 75,000 gallons. According to the Census of 1891, it would appear that the winery had 25 employees and was producing 15.4% of the provinces' wine by value, a number that would continue to increase. A report from the St. Catharines Board of Trade in 1900 commented that this winery that year handled "1,200,000 pounds of grapes which generated 100,000 gallons of wine" with the winery having storage capacity of over 200,000 gallons.

Unfortunately, Barnes would not be involved a long time with the business as he passed away on June 30, 1877. In his honour, after 1934, the winery would be renamed Barnes Wines Limited and would grow to a capacity of 1.3 million gallons making an extensive portfolio of award-winning wines. In 1988 it became part of a new winery conglomerate in the province, finally relinquishing its title of Canada's oldest operating winery.

One year after the development of the OGG&WM Co. Ltd., two lumber merchants opened a winery that they named the Niagara Falls Wine Company, even though you would be hard-pressed to see the falls from where it was located! In 1872, Francis Adam Shirriff moved to Toronto at the age of 24. Two years later, he started the Niagara Falls Wine Company with Thomas G. Bright, who already had an interest in manufacturing wine. Nine years later, Shirriff would found his own business, the Imperial Extract Company in Toronto, which he would later hand over to his three sons. Bright and Shirriff also began their winemaking in Toronto where there was a developing and handy market. They brought in grapes from Niagara and Pelee Island for the next 16 years before moving the business to Niagara Falls and establishing a large winery on Dorchester Road. Here, closer to vineyards, the winery grew quickly with sales over 50,000 gallons in the 1890's increasing to 265,000 gallons by 1910. Their success soon made them Ontario's largest winery, destined to become the leader in the industry and responsible for much of the innovation that would occur after World War II and that would drive the industry forward. Most of this would happen after the business took the name T.G. Bright and Co. Ltd. (Bright's Wines) in 1911 when the son of the founder purchased the shares held by Shirriff, who by now had earned for himself the title of "Master Marmalade Maker!" Beginning in the late 1980's, Bright's would initiate an industry consolidation of several older wineries, including

Barnes, Jordan's, Chateau Gai, and London Wineries, that would morph into a new conglomerate called Vincor, the embodiment of over 130 years of continuous Ontario winemaking!

Mention should be made of another winemaker from Toronto during the 1870's, a Toronto lawyer named John Hoskin who started growing grapes on about two acres of land north of the city in the mid 1870s. He tells us that "the Clinton and Concord are grown extensively for winemaking in Canada" at this time, but he himself preferred the Delaware grape ("free from what is called the fox") along with three other grapes that have now disappeared—the Alvey, the Creveling, and the Iona. He mentions in his presentation to the Ontario Agricultural Commission that he produced over 600 gallons of wine from his vineyard, with the best wine coming from the Iona grape. His winemaking was very straightforward. He used no machinery just manual labour. For the wine itself he used the pure juice of the grape and added just under one pound of sugar per gallon to give a little sweetness. He had his wine analyzed and found it to contain 13% alcohol, which was somewhat stronger than ordinary light wines.

For his time, John Hoskin was quite knowledgeable about the winemaking process and, although he did not make such wines himself, he believed that making second and third runs of rough, cheap wine, using water, a lot of sugar, and the grape skins from the first pressing, could be beneficial for "poorer people." He was not a commercial winemaker, but he might very well have become one, given that he had eleven first prizes from two Exhibitions— a testament to his wine's quality—and he occasionally sold a few bottles at $7 a dozen, a high price at the time. As a strong believer in the future of Ontario winemaking, John undoubtedly set a fine example for many others who were beginning to develop an interest in the fruit of the vine.

By the end of the 1870's, with wineries of various size having opened from Toronto to Niagara to Essex, one could legitimately say that Ontario had given birth to a grape and wine industry. And a beautiful baby it was! Prejudices concerning the nature of the American hybrid grapes used in making wine and in the ability to grow an increasing number of them in our cold Canadian climate had been overcome, along with the challenges of making wine in conditions that no one today would relish. The quality of the wines being made was perceived to be very good, with different wineries receiving awards in both provincial competitions and exhibitions outside Canada. And sales and consumption of local wine were increasing! At this point, as Ontario neared the end of a tremendously exciting century, the future of what was still a rather small industry looked very bright indeed.

The temperance movement was ominously gathering momentum, with producers of alcohol in its sights, but grapes themselves were not an issue. Indeed, the Concord grape in particular was actually promoted by teetotallers for its juice potential; ironically, this one grape would soon become our leading wine grape variety. Before the end of the 1870s, grapes were being planted in parts of Essex County other than Pelee, that is, around Leamington on the mainland and around the town of Sandwich near Windsor. Plantings would continue into the 1880s and 1890s, primarily of Concord grapes, but also of a variety of others including Clinton and Catawba. Overall, these plantings would reach a peak of almost 1800 acres by 1904, making Essex the third most heavily planted county in Ontario after Lincoln and Wentworth. With a significant French population in the area, it was natural that winemaking would accompany the vineyards and, indeed, several family cellars soon became de facto wineries that produced wine for family, friends, and a thirsty side clientele. Two names stand out in particular: the Girardots, who planted grapes and made wine from the mid 1870s, and the Robinets, whose involvement with grapes and winemaking would cover five decades from the 1880's on and involve three generations of the family.

Theodule (Theodore or Theodiste) Girardot was born in France in 1824 but emigrated to Sandwich early on to marry and raise a family. He became a teacher and then the principal of Assumption College for five years (1865-1870), and then public school inspector for North Essex. He also served as mayor of the town from 1873-1877. His first son, Ernest, was born in Sandwich in 1849. Like his father, he became a teacher, later also serving as mayor for 11 years, and as Commissioner of the Exhibition Branch of the Department of Agriculture.

It seems that both father and son were also very interested in viticulture and winemaking. In 1880, while working as a school inspector, Theodule provided evidence to the Agricultural Commission on the state of grape affairs in Sandwich, indicating that he had one acre of bearing grapes, but that even then there were 80-100 acres of grapes in the North Riding.

He had a few Delaware, Clinton, Rogers hybrids, and Catawba vines, but most of his vineyard was Concord. From these Concords he made 500-600 gallons of wine for his own use and to sell at about one dollar per gallon. He mentioned a cousin who was a neighbor. This cousin had two acres of grapes and sold his wine as fast as he could make it, much like Girardot "because our friends will not let us keep it long enough." He declared he sold his wine to gentlemen in the area, to doctors, and to druggists, who preferred his wine because of its purity!

At some point his son Ernest became involved and eventually a large building was constructed that bore a sign reading *Girardot Wine Co. Ltd*. According to N.F. Morrison, author of a 1964 book *Garden Gateway to Canada*, in 1890 the Ontario Deputy Minister of Agriculture visited the company vineyards when Ernest was mayor. At that time they had a 600 acre tract with most vines less than ten years old, but the wines were highly valued. In 1893 a number of Ontario wineries exhibited their wines at the Chicago Fair, including the Niagara Falls Wine Company (T.G. Bright), the Pelee Island Wine Company (J.S. Hamilton), and the E. Girardot and Company of Sandwich, which displayed clarets from 1890 and 1892, Catawbas of 1890, and sweet Burgundy and Sauterne. All entries were suitably praised! amilton)Ham

Through the 1890s, Girardot purchased sizeable amounts of grapes on several occasions from growers of Catawba on Pelee Island such as John Finlay and James Srigley. Girardot bought 40 tons in 1894, 40 in 1897, and an amazing 200 tons in 1895. The winery was still going strong in 1899 according to *The Essex County Business Directory* just one year before the passing of Theodule.

Over the next few years, winemaking was jeopardized by a reduction in local vineyards caused by grapes being replaced by plantings of tobacco. Shortly before World War I, there was a real estate boom in the area, and the Girardot vineyards were sold, and the vines left to deteriorate. By 1914 there remained only 275 acres of grapes in Essex.

Pierre Antoine Robinet ((1882-1909), like Theodule, emigrated from France, arriving in the Sandwich area in 1874. It is said that his family had five centuries of involvement in wine, and it is quite likely that this interest in winemaking brought him into contact with the Girardot family. Some form of partnership grew out of that around 1879, but it lasted only a short time as the eldest son of Pierre, Jules Robinet, who owned a brickyard in town, bought the shares of the wine-making enterprise in 1881 and started his own winery, J. Robinet and Company. Writing in 1935 about his experiences, Jules tells us that he kept the business going ever since making up to 25,000 gallons of wine each year (about 200 tons of grapes) and selling grapes to merchants in Montreal, Quebec, and Winnipeg.

In 1894-6, he expanded the business by acquiring land on Mill and Felix Streets in Sandwich that was covered with vineyards. He then built a three-storey commercial building there (still a landmark in the town to-day) with a spacious cellar for winemaking, a grocery store on the first floor, and living accommodations on the upper floors. In January of 1898, the business changed its name to J. Robinet et Freres Inc. with Jules as president and his brother Victor as vice-president.

Ever the entrepreneur, in April of 1914 he bought out his brothers' shares and proceeded to involve his sons Clovis, Joseph, Francis, Paul, and Emile, as partners in the business, now known as Robinet et fils. In 1915 he built two more stores on Sandwich Street over two large cellars and then a cellar on Talbot Road for Clovis and Francis. Five years later he turned his hand to making champagne, bringing over from France two winemakers to make "champagne" from white grapes.

In 1923 his brother Victor Robinet established his own winery, V. Robinet et fils, in Tecumseh, and Clovis opened a winery in Windsor. Francis followed in his brother's footsteps by opening a winery himself in 1926. However, the government forced him to amalgamate the operation with Francis. All of this activity, no doubt, was to take advantage of Prohibition, especially in the Windsor area, which was the gateway for much of the Canadian liquor that was making its way into Detroit. The Robinet story comes to an end in 1935 when the assets of J. Robinet et Fils were sold to the Fred Marsh Winery, those of Victor et Fils to London Winery, and those of Robinet et Freres (Clovis and Frank) to Brights. By this time, there were virtually no grapes left in Essex county. The closing of the last of the Windsor wineries, the Rossini Winery (licensed 1923) in 1938, when it was sold to the London Winery, marked a sad ending for what had been an intriguing era in Essex County.

PART FOUR

*A century of development and denial:
Ontario winemaking, 1880-1980*

Growing Pains: An industry in infancy
confronts the winds of change

> When one learns that there are already thousands of acres of vineyards in Canada and millions of dollars capital in the Dominion invested in this industry, the fine display (1893 Chicago Fair) by the wine makers of the Niagara Peninsula, as well as those in that still more favoured section of Ontario, Pelee Island in Lake Erie,... is not only what might be properly expected but would warrant an evermore representative exhibition of our country's capabilities in this line."
>
> —*Evening Record*, July 6, 1893.

Unlike the distilling industry, regulated from the start and subject to taxation soon afterwards, successive governments in Upper Canada and Ontario neither encouraged winemaking nor impeded it. Wine appears to have been considered throughout the history of the province, until 1916, as an adjunct to agriculture, rather than an industrial pursuit...

—Rannie, *Wines of Ontario.*

A pledge we make, no wine to take, nor brandy red that turns the head…so here we pledge perpetual hate to all that can intoxicate.

— Frances Willard, Women's Christian Temperance Union, 1874

the question is a difficult one … the evils flowing from the liquor traffic are very great, and it surely seems to me that it is our duty to make a strong effort to limit these evils as much as possible.

—William H. Hearst, Premier of Ontario, in a letter to Mr. Willison, April 10, 1916

Prohibition was an affront to the whole history of mankind."

—Winston Churchill

By the 1880s almost a century had passed since the beginning of pioneer settlement in the area that would come to be Ontario. In the space of these 100 years, the early colony had been transformed from virgin forest into a prosperous and thriving province with the population swelling from the few original settlers in the 1780's to over a million and a half people, and with the southern part of the province becoming fully settled.

Other changes for the better were no less dramatic in almost all aspects of life— religious, educational, economic, and political—with society quickly becoming quite self-sustaining. Economic development, which had been driven from the beginning by healthy agricultural activity and sheer hard work, only intensified with the arrival of canals, railroads, roads, the rise of a growing urban working class, and rise of the factories of the oncoming Industrial Age, offering the promise that the last decades of the 19th century would continue to improve the quality of life in Ontario.

In spite of the myriad social changes, life for women was still difficult. They continued to play only an inferior role in a patriarchal society where business and politics were dominated by men. Along with this, the consumption of what was becoming called 'booze' in daily life remained a divisive and controversial issue in a society that was literally steeped in alcohol. This, and the plight of women, found common ground in a rapidly-growing temperance movement that was part of the struggle to improve the overall quality of life—an issue that was now crying out for government attention.

With the shadow of temperance lengthening, on July 20, 1880, the Ontario Government decided to focus its sights on the developing wine industry by holding a series of interviews in nine parts of the province with people who were involved in grape and wine activities. Their "evidence" relating to grape culture and winemaking was recorded in an *Ontario Agricultural Commission Report* and released in 1881. It provided invaluable insight into all aspects of grape growing at the time. As well, it shed light on how wine was made from the grapes available, offering at the same time a wonderful array of personal opinions about which grapes to plant or to avoid and why, and which grapes made the 'best' wine.

The names of almost three-dozen different hybrid varieties appear in the report. At this time, the hybrids grew on some 400-500 acres around the province. This is an educated estimate only as government acreage statistics for these early years were not compiled Some have estimated as much as 2,000 acres! The general consensus was that the Clinton grape produced the greatest volume of wine (up to 200 gallons per ton), though the wine needed aging to drop its sharp acidity, that some grapes were much less foxy than others, like the Delaware and the Iona, and much more suitable for 'lighter' (less alcohol) dry wines, and that the Concord would grow anywhere and produce a good crop, making the most money! William Haskins, a grape grower for some 20 years and a prize-winning winemaker in Hamilton, spoke highly of the Concord as "the grape for the million," while John Hoskins Q.C. of Toronto condemned it for winemaking, declaring that it and the Clinton had given Canadian wine "a very bad name." And just about everybody loved the Catawba, if you could get it to ripen! Of all the grapes, as controversial as it was for making 'quality' wine, Concord would become the darling of the industry, the most heavily planted and the grape responsible for many different styles of wine.

Most of the other grapes mentioned in the report would shortly disappear in the province given that growers were quick to plant the grapes that were most in demand for both winemaking and market sales. And demand was increasing both locally and from as far away as Montreal and Winnipeg. The 1891 Census of Canada provides significant information about the burgeoning grape and wine industry with the provincial total for grapes, due to an increasing number of fruit growers, now reaching 4956 acres and producing some 5,800 tons of grapes – all of that within the short span of only 30 years! The Niagara Region headed the list at 1602 acres with Essex County at 1062 and Wentworth County at 849. Plantings would continue to soar to 11,100 acres in 1897 when the Ontario Bureau of Industries began to report grape acreages separately from other fruit. Such would be the direction until the early years of the new century in both the Niagara Region, where grape acreages were reported at 8,500 acres in 1911, and Essex County as we have seen, until vineyards there succumbed to the onslaught of tobacco and the rising cost of land.

The census also reported on the number of wineries operating at the time, providing a breakdown by electoral district of their production and included an analysis of their employees, male and female, over and under the age of 16. Essex County headed the list with 23 wineries out of a total of 35 in Ontario. It is interesting to note that with all its wineries, Essex produced just over 30% of the province's wine, while Niagara with only four wineries (not named) produced 50%, and Hamilton with two wineries produced 10.6% leaving about 10% for the rest of Ontario. The winery with the most employees, 25, was in all likelihood the Ontario Grape Growing and Wine Manufacturing Co. in St. Catharines whose production by now would justify that number.

Soon there were several new players in the industry such as: the winery of E.G. Brown that started in Fonthill in 1884 before selling its assets in 1906 to what became the Hillrust Wine Co. in Thorold with a cellar capacity of 150,000 gallons and the winery Robert Turner opened in Brantford in 1885 but moved to Toronto to sell its popular Turner Tonic Bitters. Before 1900 other small operations would open as well in Toronto including the Acme Wine Co. Ltd. which made unfermented wines and one operated by G.W. Peavoy as the Canadian Wine Company. Another winery was established in Niagara Falls in 1890 by the Marsh Family that would be incorporated in 1906 as the Stamford Park Wine Co. Ltd. Despite all of these, however, the total number of wineries began to fall dramatically with the removal of grapevines in Essex County, home of several small, artisanal wineries that simply ran out of grapes! And although the number of wineries in the province would bottom to a mere ten or twelve by 1916 (no one seems to be quite sure of the number), in Niagara and elsewhere, winemaking with the same American hybrid grapes carried on. Niagara alone, in 1909, was recorded as using 2400 tons of grapes, which would have produced approximately 350,000 gallons of wine!

But in 1916 it would be easy to believe that the wine industry might be on the ropes, not because of the nature or quality of the wine itself, but because of the rising tide of a Temperance movement that was given even more impetus by the outbreak of World War I. Indeed, it appeared that the wine industry, along with the brewing and distilling businesses, would become a victim of Prohibition.

At the beginning of its first 50 years of commercial availability in the province, native wine, even though often quite high in alcohol, was rarely associated with excessive drinking and related evils, and was more often considered as a healthful drink of moderation with the potential to actually promote temperance. Certainly, wine was considered less likely to cause drunkenness than other forms of alcohol, and was viewed as more of a medicine or a tonic, as well as ideal for sacramental use. Thus wine had received much less attention from temperance advocates as the cause of the working man's ills. But as the century wore on, with increasing temperance activity demanding better overall living conditions with the eradication of "booze," the idea of a totally alcohol-free society became more and more popular, and the threat of the province going 'dry' became very real for the entire alcohol business. Indeed, south of the border many American wineries were closing because of the prevailing temperance mood, and their vineyards were left to decay.

With the passage of the Dunkin Act in the United Province of Canada of 1864 that allowed any county or municipality to prohibit the retail sale of liquor by a majority vote, and with the passage of the Canada Temperance Act of 1878 (also known as the Scott Act), which extended through the use of plebiscite the 'local option' to all of Canada, the government signaled its awareness of the public's concern about alcoholic beverages. This latter act had followed closely on the formation in 1874 in Owen Sound of the first Prohibition Women's League to force the removal of liquor licences from grocery stores (by 1874 Ontario had more than 6,000 outlets for alcoholic beverages), and in 1877 of the Women's Christian Temperance Union that sought "total abstinence from all things harmful" by pressuring government to enact legislation that would curtail the abuse of alcohol. In Ontario in 1892 a Royal Commission travelled cross-country to take the public pulse on pro-prohibitionist legislation and to establish the impact this would have on industry, the economy, and on society. Despite all of the questions posed and answers received, no actions were taken due to the fear of inflicting damage on the local economy. By 1895 Canada-wide sales of spirits had reached 3.8 million gallons along with 17.4 million gallons of beer with wine sales a distant third at only 512,000 gallons, a mere 2% of alcohol sold – all in all clear evidence of the prodigious amount of drinking in the country.

In 1898, the federal government held a national prohibition plebiscite that finally provided a victory for the prohibitionists, but Sir Wilfrid Laurier refused to make this legal as the vote was so close (51.3% for and 48.7% against) and Quebec had voted overwhelmingly against it (81.2%). And the Ontario government twice held plebiscites, in 1894 and 1902, to control or eliminate the sale of alcohol in Ontario, which both failed in spite of considerable support. Yet for temperance zealots the trend was indeed a friend. Parts of Ontario started to go dry under local option (the number rose from 187 districts in 1905 to 520 in 1914) with store licences declining from 1,307 in 1875 to 298 in 1905 and to only 218 by 1914 and with tavern licenses falling to 1,371 in 1914 from an awesome 4,794 in 1875.

The outbreak of World War I in August, 1914 brought the matter of prohibition in Ontario to a head and would serve as the catalyst for the ultimate political decision that the Conservatives had been delaying. After the sudden death of Premier Sir James Whitney, who never favoured more than moderate restrictive legislation, William H. Hearst, an active Methodist and strong temperance advocate, became premier in September. At first he and his party, still concerned about any negative economic impact that total Prohibition would have on the province, moved cautiously, reducing slightly the hours of operation of liquor shops and distributors. This was followed in 1915 by legislation to establish a new, centralized Liquor License Commission to replace the local commissioners and a new restriction on bars until the end of the war that would have them close three hours earlier at night.

Under the guise of unselfish patriotism—their self-denial apparently showed sympathy for soldiers who were sacrificing their lives overseas—the prohibitionists began to argue that alcohol should be diverted to benefit the war effort, a move that would result, they said, in greater efficiency in the workplace. In the throne speech in 1916, the government finally gave in to public sentiment and announced that a bill would be introduced shortly detailing the government's position.

When it was presented in March, Bill 100 stipulated that all bars, taverns, clubs, and shops would have to close for the duration of the war (after which a referendum on their future would be held), and the sale of intoxicating liquor would become illegal except for medicinal, mechanical, scientific, artistic, or sacramental use. The manufacture of liquor and its importation into Ontario would remain unchanged, as these were both under federal jurisdiction (although shortly afterwards, on April 1st, 1918, they too would be prohibited by a federal Order-in-Council). It would be perfectly legal, however, to consume alcoholic beverages in the privacy of one's own home! Although many in Hearst's party were not happy, the Ontario Temperance Act came into effect on Sunday, September 17th, 1916, passing unanimously and changing overnight the social landscape of Ontario.

Considering the importance of the grape-growing industry to the province and considering the plight of farmers with vineyards that could not simply cease production, the government made an exception for wine made from native grapes by Ontario wineries, legalizing the sale of wine in pharmacies for 'medical use' and from a winery's single on-site retail store, as long as the consumer purchased at the winery a minimum of five gallons (two cases) at one time.

The impact of this decision on the Ontario wine industry would be dramatic.

After the passing of the O.T.A. a number of individuals soon appreciated the opportunity presented by the legislation, to make and sell the only legal alcoholic beverage in Ontario by opening a licensed winery, a loophole which temperance activists tried in vain to close, but which numerous entrepreneurs turned to their advantage! In 1918 wineries opened from Niagara to Windsor to Fort William with a licence to make Ontario wine almost without restriction. One year later there were 20 winery licences in effect, a number that would increase to over 50 by 1925 many appearing overnight in basements, cellars, backyards, and barnyards, with "improper and unsanitary quarters and inadequate equipment."

Proliferating like rabbits, wineries opened all over the province, from Northern Ontario to Toronto, Kitchener, Guelph, Oakville, Burlington, in places where there were no grapes at all, and several more in the Windsor area and in the Hamilton to Niagara region. Many wineries simply took the name of the licence holder, as A. de Conza and sons, Franco Cerra Winery, Rossini's, Rosie Dibbley Wine Co., Subosits. Others were named after their location including the Beamsville Winery, the Thorold Winery, the Jordan Wine Co., the Sudbury Wine Co., the Twin City Winery, and the Hamilton Winery, while others were named with more creativity such as The Old Fort Wine Co., Peerless, the Niagara Cataract Native Winery, and Beaverdam Cataract Winery. To add to the confusion, licences were issued and lost so that the actual total could not be verified, while other licences changed hands, and some wineries changed locations, and even unlicensed operations sprung up in the pursuit of profit with no one providing proper oversight.

A government report that appeared just a few years after the repeal of Prohibition, presented by the Ontario Wine Standards Committee, was extremely critical of the number of winery licences that were issued after 1916 by the newly appointed provincial Board of Commissioners, stating that the board granted licences without "exercising sufficient care" to establish the winemaking credentials or competency of the applicants or examining their production facilities. It concluded that "a number of permits came into the possession of men who should never have been permitted under a government licence to sell to the public the product of their manufacture."

Little wonder that the Prohibition era has gone down in our history as "chaos," or "a misguided attempt at social control," or "a nightmare" peopled, by rum-runners, smugglers, bootleggers, corrupt officials, and those who made their own moonshine or bath-tub gin, or drank unlawfully in speakeasies or the so-called blind pigs; in short, a time when nefarious activities of all sorts proliferated. Surprisingly, arrests for public drunkenness, alcohol-related deaths and associated crimes actually declined over the time.

Not surprisingly, the consumption of 'legal' native wine soared from some 222,000 gallons in Canada at the beginning of the 1920's to over 2,200,000 gallons in Ontario alone just ten years later, a reflection of its privileged status. Indeed, considering the downsizing of the industry just prior to the legislation taking effect, one could legitimately wonder if this kind of growth in sales would ever have happened without the impetus of Prohibition. But it was the scandalous quality of much of the wine produced, and not the volume, that would be remembered in the years that followed, leaving an indelible stain on the reputation of our native wine.

While some of the permits ended up in "satisfactory hands," with so many in the Prohibition era industry lacking proper facilities, equipment and basic winemaking expertise, and with virtually no inspections, government controls, or enforcement to rein in the neophytes, there were bound to be problems. The result was too much wine of abysmal quality, such as a form of alcohol laced with vinegar (acetic acid/volatile acidity), and cloudy concoctions that had re-fermented in the bottle or bottles with unsightly sediment.

Often winemaking methods were near criminal, with grapes that on average produce 150 gallons of juice to the ton being stretched with the addition of water (euphemistically called 'amelioration') to three or four times the volume and chaptalized with the addition of tons of sugar to produce the desired alcohol. Unhealthy, even carcinogenic products, were added to restore or enhance colour, or to stabilize and preserve the wine. This was the time in our winemaking history when even Catawba, a highly-prized grape "became a bad name," in William Rannie's words, given that many wineries appropriated it for their cheapest and poorest quality wine.

Many writers have shown how such winemaking over the 11 years of Prohibition almost proved a death-blow to the industry, but none more colourfully than Percy Rowe, who commented in 1970 in his book *The Wines of Canada* that "Prohibition changed a combination of good husbandry and gentle craft into a monster whose products were so poor that it seemed bent on a form of mass suicide. "But it was Prohibition as a whole that was failing the province and the sorry state of Ontario's native wines was just one aspect of this failure. In 1924 a referendum was held to determine if the Ontario Temperance Act should be continued just five years after another referendum had solidly dismissed the notion of repeal of Prohibition and the sales of spirits in government stores. It passed but by a very close vote of 51.5% to 48.5%, indicating a significant change in public favour.

Two years later the Conservatives won the election with a promise to repeal Prohibition.

Fortunately, self-destruction was not to be the fate of the wine industry despite the denigration of "Ontario wine" at this time, and it must be said, in all fairness to the industry, that much acceptable wine was actually being made during this period by a number of valid wineries, including both well-established operations and a number that had opened during Prohibition.

J.S. Hamilton in Brantford, the Robinets in Sandwich, Hillrust, Barnes in St. Catharines, and Stamford Park and Brights in Niagara Falls had all proven to be competent wineries and continued to produce a range of ports and sherries that set the bar for quality in Ontario winemaking for the era with Brights, the largest winery, developing the first production bottling line in Canada in 1924. And among the plethora of newcomers that arrived during the 1920s, two additional operations emerged as solid businesses that would go on to make a significant contribution to the industry.

In 1925 London Winery Ltd. was founded by an electrical engineer, A.K. Knowles, who had established the largest electrical contracting business in Western Ontario. After purchasing the assets and licence held by Giovanni Paproni of Welland (1922), he provided additional financing for the new winery, believing that Prohibition would soon be coming to an end. His brother, J.C. Knowles, had been working at his father-in-law's winery in Oakville and after it was sold he moved to London to become the new winemaker or "chemist" as winemakers were called then. As President, A.K. Knowles would lead a family winery with intentions of producing only quality wine. Indeed, over the following years, London would become an asset to the industry, generating numerous winemaking innovations from the use of flor yeast in sherry production and the introduction of Millipore filtration, to the marketing of wine in decanters and plastic bottles.

The Jordan Wine Company also originated in the mid 1920s when a Scottish distiller named William B. Cleland bought a company called Canadian Grape Products that was established in what had originally been an apple-drying plant in the tiny village of Jordan, a few miles to the west of St. Catharines. That business had evolved into a grape juice plant and then a producer of jams, jellies, ciders, and cider vinegar that came to be owned by two partners: Archibald J. Haines and W.H. Aikens. In 1920 it was licenced to make wine and produced a fine sparkling wine it called Gold Seal Champagne. Four years later Cleland bought the business, changing the name to the Jordan Wine Company and soon after purchased the Welch's grape juice plant in St. Catharines where the winery would later move. Like London Winery, Jordan's would build a solid reputation for its popular, high-alcohol sherries and ports.

Unfortunately, in spite of good winemaking practices on the part of so many wineries, the reputation of our native wines from the era remains scandalous to this day, all tarred with the same sordid brush. In a way, the government had been responsible for this, and in the spring of 1927 it would be the government that would end the reign of the "monster" it had created.

Changing the game: Control, clean-up, consolidation, ...and Chardonnay!

> I think the Concord is perhaps the most profitable for market, because the public have little taste...
>
> —Arnold, *Ontario Agricultural Commission Report*, 1881.
>
> So while to-day most people laugh at or vilify the Prohibition impulse as...seriously damaging to the reputation of Ontario wine, a positive outcome emerged from this era. Its weaknesses created a situation that strengthened and expanded viable wine businesses.
>
> —Malleck, *The World of Niagara Wine*
>
> ...behind the wine industry and always recognized is the widespread interest of the grape growers. The Board would like to see that interest conserved and proper profits secured by the growers. The Board's merchandising of native wines all over the province has very greatly enhanced the interest of the grape growers and greatly advantaged grape growing.
>
> *Sessional Papers of Ontario*, 1931.

> Whatever his reasons, Harry Hatch brought his resources to bear in his quest to make better wines. Harry's ambition inspired the turnaround of the Ontario wine industry.
>
> —Bramble, *Niagara's Wine Visionaries,*.

April 1927 witnessed the opening of a new chapter in Ontario alcohol history with the demise of Prohibition and the arrival of the Liquor Control Act, which replaced denial with control as the law of the land. A Liquor Control Board was immediately created with responsibility for all aspects of the alcohol business in the province from quality assurance to distribution and consumption, including marketing and sales in the new retail store system.

A major part of their mandate was to deal with Ontario wine, now a mainstream product distinct from beer and spirits, and capable of generating valuable revenue on its own but suffering from a lack of credibility as a quality product. And behind the wine industry were Ontario growers whose grapes were still considered important to the province's economy. Going forward, the LCBO would take a "personal interest in the affairs of the grape growers" and attempt to establish a fair price for grapes in the province—a policy that persists to this day. Thus, wasting no time, the government immediately introduced what would become the first of many support programs, a serious attempt to put these industries back on a sound footing, by initiating a series of regulatory changes that would address the nature of all winemaking in the province.

As a first step, the LCBO joined forces with the Department of Health to tackle issues relating to winery hygiene and wine quality. Wineries were now to be inspected and wines analyzed. The government also set up winemaking classes to help improve the knowledge and skills of any winemakers who were interested in showing up. To eradicate all sub-standard wines from sale, the LCBO refused to accept any Ontario product for its new store system unless it was free from sediment, turbidity, or artificial flavours, and had a satisfactory colour and pleasing character. This was a step to address wine refermention due to yeasts and bacteria remaining in the wine, broken bottles, and wines with foreign matter in them, all of which was the result of poor winemaking. Even more problematic were wines with terribly high levels of volatile acidity—an obvious taste of vinegar caused by spoilage bacteria. New regulations that reduced such acidity to .2%, a marked improvement over former days, curtailed overnight the activity of several dubious wineries that could not match such standards. And a ceiling of 250 gallons of wine from a ton of grapes was established to limit the practice of creating wine from water and sugar and then adding numerous unhealthy additives in the pursuit of volume over anything else.

Accompanying these restrictions was a change in the law to allow other viable wineries, to buy up the assets of those going out of business—at prices approved by the LCBO— and acquire the right with the purchased licence to open another retail store in a location of their choosing anywhere in Ontario. This helped several wineries to grow their business in the face of new competition from the rapidly expanding LCBO retail store system (now offering imported wines for sale again in the 80 new stores that opened) that was having a negative impact on on-site winery sales. At the same time, the government decided to close the door on the opening of any new wineries, limiting the licences to the 51 in existence—a policy that would stay in effect until the 1960's.

Many fledgling wineries that had opened all over the province during Prohibition to serve a purely local trade would end their days in mergers and acquisitions by other more established wineries. The story of Dominic Depietro, a Toronto grocer, is typical of winery activity at the time. Dominic had bought a grape farm in the early 1920's in the Beamsville area where he converted a pig barn into a wine cellar. His Concord wine was a bargain at 50 cents a gallon and he developed a following. In 1928, after just five years doing business, he sold his assets to other promoters and the winery moved to Fort Erie, a short boat ride across from the illegal but thirsty Buffalo market, where it became the Old Fort Wine Company. The Old Fort licence was sold to Bright's in 1939. In Kitchener, Fred Kampman obtained a licence to make wine in his basement. He operated successfully for eight years, selling a Catawba White, Concord, and a red wine, all made in barrels from a rather crude blending of first and second runs, water, and sugar—all unfiltered! He sold his operation in 1930 to the H. Robinson Corporation of Hamilton. After a bankruptcy, the Robinson Winery ended business in1937 in the manner of so many other wineries, by being sold to Brights.

Another enterprise that dates to 1928 became a success in spite of the difficult environment at that time, and like London and Jordan wineries would develop into a very well-known brand. In that year a former newspaperman named Alex G. Sampson led the amalgamation of 6 wineries into a new company called Canadian Wineries Ltd., taking over the Stamford Park winery in Niagara Falls, which had only two years earlier acquired the assets of the old CVGA in Cooksville, and four other recently established wineries. The new company now consisted of the Peerless Winery in Toronto, incorporated in 1925 after buying the licence of Antonio Nero (1922), The Dominion Wine Growers in Oakville (1919), Lincoln Wines in St. Catharines (1925) and the Thorold Winery started by Nicola Pataracchia in 1922 as well as Stamford Park. One year later it would absorb a sixth winery, National Wines of Toronto that had been incorporated in 1922.

Almost immediately Canadian Wineries purchased the patent rights for Canada for the "Methode Charmat" sparkling wine process which would allow it to make sparkling wines and "champagne" in a novel, bulk format as opposed to the traditional second fermentation in the bottle. Canadians would come to know the company by a new name in 1940 when it became Chateau Gai, using the name of its top-selling Canadian champagne for the winery name itself.

The end of Prohibition marked a challenging time for many Ontario wineries now faced with increasing competition from the alcohol and brewing industries as well as the new government stores. In addition, government control kept consumption of alcohol under tight rein in spite of a new and respectable attitude to drinking that was evolving. Unfortunately, the depression of the 1930's itself further curtailed consumer spending. And, although the government continued to encourage Ontario grape growing and wine production, the latter now faced new regulations and standards that proved impossible for any makeshift operation to achieve. The result was an immediate and rapid decline in the number of wineries that through the 1930's would see over 20 smaller operations disappear into history after selling their assets to another winery that was happy to obtain their retail licence. At the same time, through this consolidation of ownership, a much smaller number of wineries began to transform into corporations, mass producing wine in much larger facilities.

One such operation started in Toronto in 1930 through the purchasing of the 1921 licence of Fort William winemaker Franco Cerra, and by then buying other wineries including Lakeshore, the Regal Wine Co, and Beaverdam Cataract Winery. The venture was renamed Danforth Wines in 1938 and endured until 1964 when its assets were sold to Jordan's.

Another successful venture that blossomed in the 30's, The Parkdale Winery, began business in the cellar of Toronto Rabbi Jacob Gordon producing Passover wine in the early 1920's. The licence was purchased shortly after by the Oporto Wine Co. and then the Concord Wine Co. in Toronto. In 1936 the Concord Wine Co. changed its named to Parkdale Wines Ltd. and began to acquire the assets of other wineries including the Hamilton Winery in 1938, Acme Wines in 1954, and Grimsby Wines Ltd. in 1966. Although the winery disappeared shortly after, for a long time in Ontario Parkdale wines were very popular supported by their winery advertising slogan which encouraged consumers to "pick a Parkdale" for any occasion.

The last of the new wineries would arrive in 1969, again by a process of acquisitions that started in Fonthill in 1930 and became The Welland Winery when the assets were transferred to the defunct Subosits Winery there. The winery remained in business until 1964 when it was sold to the Imperial Tobacco Company and moved to Winona becoming Beau Chatel Wines. Six years later the business would be sold again to Andrew Peller, an ambitious entrepreneur who had started his wine career in British Columbia and was now expanding to Ontario.

The opening of the appropriately named Andres Wines marked the end of 40 years of a clean-up and consolidation in the Ontario wine industry that had produced a dramatic change in the winery landscape. Where there had once been over 40 small and often marginal operations along with a small number of experienced wineries, by 1970 only seven large wineries remained in business: Barnes, Brights, Chateau Gai, Jordans, London, Turner's and the newly-named Andres, transformed into a group of corporate winemakers selling their products locally in LCBO stores and in their own retail store networks as well as across Canada and abroad.

That anyone in the early 1930's would have been able to sense this renaissance that was in store for the grape and wine industry would have been difficult to believe. Sales of Ontario wines and wine consumption began to drop as a result of a depressed economy in the so-called dirty thirty's with the world enduring what came to be called the Great Depression, leaving many grape growers on the verge of bankruptcy, and forcing the government to provide additional assistance by establishing a minimum price for grapes, $40 a ton, that wineries would now be obligated to pay growers. And in 1931, to further help the sale of Ontario grapes, the government allowed an enhanced fortification of wines with Ontario grape spirit to enable wineries to produce ports and sherries similar to European imports with their higher alcohol levels. This also allowed the wineries to distill volumes of poor wine that was still in tanks for use in producing fortified products, rather than just discarding the wine, while grapes not needed for wine could still be purchased for distillation. At the same time, the government legislated a ban on the importation of grapes from outside Ontario, again to support the growers. Taxes were further reduced on wine, lowering the price of some to just thirty cents a bottle to assist impecunious consumers, a price which would help stabilize sales.

Throughout Prohibition, wineries had become adept at creating products by natural fermentations that generated up to 18% alcohol, which they required in the ubiquitous ports and sherries of the Ontario industry. The only problem with this was that fermentations usually finished around 13% alcohol even with abundant sugar remaining and winemakers were truly challenged to restart the stalled process. In reminiscing about his long career in the industry as a winemaker at Chateau Gai, Edwin R. Haynes provided remarkable details about fermenting with natural yeasts at that time in these words: "during fermentation you prayed to the tank, you cursed the tank, you kicked the side of it, you heated it, you added ammonium phosphate, you added urea, and if anyone had any other ideas you tried that too. The highest alcohol that I've ever heard of by natural fermentation was one by Gerry Kavanaugh at Turner's Winery in Toronto when they got up to 23½ percent alcohol by natural fermentation." Winemakers today would be very skeptical about reaching such levels (although they no longer use the carcinogenic urea as a yeast nutrient) but these were verified at the time by the LCBO laboratory. The talent of some of these winemakers has to be appreciated, for they did not have the use of the cultured and freeze-dried yeasts available to winemakers today and had to continually build their yeasts from agar slants month by month in their winery laboratory—a difficult and demanding task!

Other aspects of winemaking then would also not be welcomed by our current cadre of winemakers who have a broad range of wonderful *vinifera* grapes to choose from. Mr. Hayes described the choice he had: "When we started we had Concords, Niagaras, Catawbas, (that was all that growers wanted to grow) and if you were lucky, a few Delawares. From these grapes you had to make everything, from champagne to vermouth and everything in between." And winemaking conditions were still quite rustic, if not primitive. The fermenters were huge: 16-to-18-feet in diameter, and about five feet high. The winemaker stood on planks that were set across the tank and used a 12-foot-long plunger to punch down the cap for hours on end. Many a winemaker went for a swim! Eventually pumps were used to pump the must over the cap, but the heat and build-up of carbon dioxide from the fermentation would have been extreme. To cool these massive 60,000-gallon tanks a block and tackle system was used (no glycol refrigeration units!) to haul a 100-pound block of ice up to the top of the tank where it was dropped in to the 100 F. degree fermentation. Later they devised a system of pumping the wine over ice in a smaller tank that could be loaded with ice directly from a truck. In any case, a little more water in the wine did not seem to bother anyone!

With changes in the industry, the government had been hopeful that the wineries would now start to make lighter, less intoxicating wines with lower alcoholic content, wines more suitable for consumption with meals, along the lines of many imported table wines. But the new, fortified category at 30% alcohol proved immediately popular with consumers who were able to drown their troubles with these inexpensive soothers. By 1933 they were accounting for over a 40% share of the market. However, to protect the public, a new regulation would limit claret type wines to 13% alcohol. Meanwhile, the notorious medicated and tonic wines sold in drug stores were virtually eliminated when the government obligated an additive in their formulation that would induce vomiting if this drugstore wine was consumed in excess.

To further discourage consumption, the government made the buying experience in their liquor stores totally uninviting, bothersome and restrictive. Consumers required a permit to buy, and could not touch the product before purchase. And limits were set on the amount of any purchase—in the case of wine, one gallon per day!—although a store manager could refuse to sell to anyone he considered a problem drinker. I still have a fond memory of my father visiting an LCBO outlet on Concession Street in Hamilton in the 1950s, using his permit for the purchase and receiving the product from the employee in a brown paper bag with the warning not to open it for drinking until we reached our own home.

During this period, Ontario wines tended to be sweet to help balance high grape acidity levels. They were most often red in colour and, in Tony Aspler's words, "closer to whisky than wine in their alcoholic strength." The top-selling style of wine was sherry, followed by various versions of port that, in a tradition dating back to the 1860's, was often some form of blend that precluded vintage dating. Other wine styles simply used European names, like Claret for reds, Sauternes for white, and Champagne for sparkling wines.

Grape growing, as well, was traditional, featuring solely North American hybrids (due to the ongoing inability of European *viniferas* to adapt to our environment), usually categorized as *labrusca*, with the much-maligned Concords, and the greenish-coloured Niagara variety representing over 80% of vineyard plantings. Both grapes were associated with the musk-like flavour described as foxiness; that is, a potent grapey character, one that many found offensive in native wines, and which was difficult to eliminate. Wineries tried a variety of means to reduce this undesirable element, using oxidation and heat to produce sherries, or sweetening to bring wines into a flavour balance, or alcohol and aging for ports.

Today such native wines have lost all popularity, if not credibility, but remarkably, a sizeable industry was able to maintain itself selling these styles of wine almost exclusively. Almost all wineries had their own retail store networks led by Brights, with some fourteen stores, one for each licence acquired after Prohibition and London Winery with eight stores. The largest of the wineries remaining in business would eventually open wineries in other provinces to improve their retail status there. Any discussion of Ontario wine made in the 30 years following the end of Prohibition usually centres on the dubious quality of the wine—from our present-day vantage point—but consumers continued to buy them, and in significant volumes, making these businesses attractive acquisition targets by larger companies. Beginning in the 1950's various distillers and brewers would take an interest in the industry with Seagrams swallowing up Jordan-Danforth (later sold to

O'Keefe Brewery) and Hiram Walker absorbing Brights. A few years later, John Labatt Brewery would acquire Chateau-Gai; Barnes would eventually be sold to the British distiller, Gilbey's.

For winemaking, the characteristics of these grapes dictated the kinds of wine being made, almost anything except elegant dry wine. Moreover, the notion that quality wine is made in the vineyard was still at least half a century in the future. Instead, growers followed what might be called a simplistic "plant and pick" regime, seeking as many tons to the acre as possible with little concern for grape quality or even sugar levels (not normally high in most of these varieties to begin with) which could be adjusted in the winery in any case.

In short, the vast majority of Ontario grown grapes were simply not suitable for the production of good quality table wines like those coming from Europe, but that did not matter to most consumers who were accustomed to the standard Ontario wine profile, and who felt no need for any change, nor did it matter to most wineries, who were content to satisfy public demand. An LCBO analysis completed in 1946, indicated that only 0.5% of wines sold at that time represented the table wine category, a category that would not become truly popular until several years after the Second World War.

Although the demand for lighter alcohol table wines in the 1930s was low, some individuals in the industry believed that the potential of our native grapes was indeed limited, and that it was time to improve on the varieties of grapes in use by the industry. A revised program was underway at the Vineland Horticultural Experimental Station in the mid 30s to create new grapes that would prove hardy and sustainable for growers and make better wine. In fact, as early as 1923 the Research Station abandoned the use of Niagara and Concord grapes in their grape breeding program attempting to produce more *vinifera*-type grapes and create thousands of seedlings. But such hybridization, cross-breeding, maturing, and evaluating hundreds of wines, would prove a slow process, with little to show for all the dedicated efforts, and history would have to find another catalyst if any significant change was to happen. The year 1933 would provide just that and prove to be a defining moment for winemaking in the province, an unheralded dawning of a new era for Ontario grapes and wine.

In that year, a man named Harry Hatch, who had made a large fortune during Prohibition as the so-called King of Canadian Distillation, bought

T.G. Bright and Company in Niagara Falls from William Bright, son of Thomas Bright, the winery's founder. Although this was Canada's largest winery, with a 4,000,000 gallon capacity, people wondered why, at this challenging time, Harry would want to buy a winery that made mainly sherries and ports. Linda Bramble makes a telling comment about their wines in her book *Niagara's Wine Visionaries*, noting that William liked to brag about never drinking his own wines, one of which was popularly called "Bright's disease"!

To his credit, Harry Hatch quickly implemented a business plan to bring needed improvements to his company's wines and to restore sagging sales—changes that would eventually result in a revolution in Ontario winemaking. In 1934, Brights purchased 1,400 acres of Niagara and Concord grapes, and initiated his own vineyard program with Jacob Hostetter as the vineyard manager. A new winemaking team was hired, led by an American, Dr. John Eoff, who had been working in California at a company called Fruit Industries Ltd., and a Frenchman named Adhemar de Chaunac, who had experience working in sugar refineries and with a yeast-making firm in Quebec. Both men were microbiologists, with expertise in quality control and winemaking, and they set about modernizing the winery with De Chaunac named chief chemist. When evaluating the company wines, De Chaunac is said to have remarked that the red wines were "sweet" and the white wines "undrinkable," motivating Harry Hatch to initiate a grape-research program directed at improved winemaking.

For dry wines, De Chaunac first experimented with the American hybrid varieties that lacked obvious foxiness—Delaware, Catawba, Agawam and Elvira. In 1941 he released the first new Ontario table wine since Prohibition: Manor St. David's Sauternes. The work so impressed Hatch that he sent De Chaunac to France to investigate better varieties. These consisted of new hybrid grapes that had been created over the previous half-century by French hybridizers as one means of combatting the *Phylloxera* crisis. In France these *vinifera/non-labrusca* North American hybrid crosses had proven popular as hardy, disease-resistant vines that produced good crops, with nearly half a million acres planted there prior to 1930. A small number of these hybrids, bearing only the name of their creator and a number such as Seibel 9549, had already made their way to New York State by this time with more to arrive from France during the 1930's and 1940s until the Second World War stopped their export.

De Chaunac became aware of these hybrids (usually called French Hybrids or French-American Hybrids as a group) and their winemaking potential through an association with a small group of colleagues from the Geneva Research Station in New York State and two wineries there. He declared that a wine he himself made from Seibel 1000 (the grape was named Rosette in 1970) was "the first acceptable quality red in Canada." Tastings of wines made from the hybrids led those in the group to realize that they had the potential to make very good dry table wine, and the decision was made by Bright's to establish commercial plantings as soon as they could obtain vines. After Dr. Eoff died in 1940, De Chaunac was appointed Director of Research with a new assistant, George Hostetter, and together these two men continued the pursuit of improved grapes and wines for the winery.

For the years before and during World War II, the Ontario wine industry essentially marked time with fewer wineries, and it would not be until near the end of the war that sales once again approached the three-and-a-half million gallons of 1930. This time, there was no second Prohibition to assist sales, only a rationing of supplies and low sales to add to the challenges of war-time production. Sugar was difficult to obtain, and it became more expensive. Difficulties in obtaining bottles meant that wineries had to recycle them, and it was a challenge to obtain closures for bottles. According to the *Report of the LCBO* of 1948, sales in Ontario decreased by about 7% from 1939 to 1945. However, total sales of Ontario wine managed to increase from 2,695,076 gallons just before the war to 3,922,110 in 1946, with almost half of the production being exported to other provinces and elsewhere. And the industry could be proud of impressive sales that reached over four million gallons in 1947 with just over two million sold in the province!

At the conclusion of the war, De Chaunac once again visited France to select a number of the more suitable French hybrids. He chose some 200 vines each of 35 numbered varieties like Seibel 9549, 10878, and 9110, as well as a few *vinifera* vines (including Chardonnay and Pinot Noir) for trial plantings in Bright's vineyards. In 1947 he arranged for a similar selection to be sent to the Horticultural Research Station in Vineland. Two hundred cuttings of Seibel 9549 were rooted and a row of 150 vines was planted in the experimental vineyard at Vineland in 1948. These vines proved to be hardy and wine made from this grape showed well in blind tastings. In December, 1953, Brights Wines obtained 300 cuttings for planting the following year, starting the grape on its way to becoming the most widely planted varietal in Canada (in 1977, 6292 tons of Seibel 9549/ De Chaunac would be purchased by Ontario wineries). Not all plantings were successful, but some of the varieties not only grew well but also showed good potential for making dry wine with a European character. Bright's made the decision to begin commercial plantings of the French hybrids, and 40,000 vines were planted in 1948. A year later De Chaunac came out with a blend of two French hybrids: Seibel 10878 and Seibel 1000. This latter was called Manor St. David's Claret. It was the first French hybrid wine to be produced commercially in Canada. He also produced a bottle-fermented champagne called President, a blend that included American and French hybrid varieties.

In 1951 Bright's made the first commercial planting of *vinifera* in Canada with a ten-acre vineyard of Chardonnay. George Hostetter had discovered that with a proper spraying program to control mildew, and by using rootstocks more resistant to *Phylloxera*, it was possible to grow grapes like Pinot Noir and Chardonnay with some success. Harry Hatch had passed away in 1946. T.G. Bright's, however, after testing hundreds of varieties in their experimental programs, continued to invest nearly $2,000,000 in expanded plantings, while at the same time providing research stations, nurseries, and other wineries with cuttings, and encouraging their growers to plant the new varieties, all while providing professional viticultural assistance to them. In Bright's experimental vineyards under the direction of George Hostetter, the winery tested some 500 grape varieties and developed a superior clone of Baco Noir, which came to be known as George's Clone, a fitting tribute to the dedicated Mr. Hostetter! Indeed, one has to wonder where the Ontario Wine Industry would be today if Harry Hatch had not bought Bright's Wines and followed through on his commitment to improve our winemaking.

From this courageous and dedicated beginning, Bright's produced Canada's first *vinifera* wine in 1955, a Canadian champagne labeled Pinot, and followed this in 1956 with the first varietal, which they called Pinot Chardonnay. Today it is considered incorrect to use the word Pinot with Chardonnay; but, after all, this was a first effort!. Two years later they would upset the French (who supplied the original Marechal Foch vines for the wine) by labeling a new product that was made from Foch grapes as Canadian Burgundy. By this time in France, there were almost 1,000,000 acres planted in French hybrid grapes. These had proven popular for being hardier, more resistant to *Phylloxera*, and more productive than the sensitive *vinifera*. Still, some Frenchmen considered them "bastards" since these hybrids had a unique flavour that was not as elegant or refined as the *vinifera*. They called them American hybrids and encouraged efforts to curtail their use in French table wine. Now someone had dared to call an Ontario wine Burgundy that was crafted from these hybrid grapes! There would be more upset to follow!

These initial efforts would be just a hint of more progress to come, but they coincided with societal developments from which they stood to benefit, and which would drive our winemaking as a whole forward from Prohibition-era inertia to meaningful change. Yet even at this time, many growers were still skeptical about planting the new grapes (especially the *vinifera*, which had a 300-year plus history of failure in Eastern North America), while others believed it would be better to experiment at the Horticultural Research Institute of Ontario in Vineland in order to produce more suitable hybrids locally. While several new grapes like Vincent, Veeblanc, Ventura, and Veeport were developed at the H.R.I.O beginning in the 1950s and into the 1960s, the efforts of the dedicated crew at Chateau "V" led by the legendary Oliver (Ollie) A. Bradt and winemaker Ralph Crowther would prove of little value for the industry as a whole in comparison to the experimentation with the French hybrids. One of the grapes developed is now called Acadie Blanc and, although it really never became popular in Ontario, it has found an appropriate home in Nova Scotia where it is producing some top quality wines.

It would take just a few more years to establish that the new varieties would grow and survive in our environment and to convince farmers, who naturally were reluctant to pull out needed grapes vines, that they could make a better return on the hybrids and *viniferas*, since they sold for more than the standard varieties. With that realization, beginning in the 1960s—and although the older grapes still had a role to play—the writing was on the wall for the future of viticulture in Ontario; indeed, the time was rapidly coming when it would be necessary to leave the past behind.

Ontario Native wine in the 60s and 70s: transitioning from adolescence towards obsolescence

> Our Citizens desire, subject to reasonable controls, to be able to purchase alcoholic beverages in convenient and pleasant surroundings without feeling that they are committing any wrongdoing.
>
> —Grossman, Commissioner of the LCBO, 1961

> The purchase of Beau Chatel winery by Andrew Peller when Concord was coming out of our ears, was a godsend to the Ontario grape industry. Until Andres hit the market our wines were dead!
>
> —Wiley, former Chairman, Ontario Grape Growers' Marketing Board

> Only in Canada is it a national pastime for everyone to dump on all our domestic wines and to drink instead any cheap European import as long as the label looks foreign and the name is unpronounceable.
>
> —Aspler, *Vintage Canada*, 1983.

> Perhaps it is not too much to hope that the best days of the specialist, the small individual wine maker producing superior wines for an increasingly sophisticated clientele, still lie in the future.
>
> —Rannie, *Wines of Ontario*, 1977.

With the arrival of the 1960s the Ontario wine industry began to encounter headwinds that would eventually cause it to change direction after a prolonged adolescence spent in the shadow of the Concord grape. For years, the industry had made little progress in improving overall wine quality. Still, Ontario wines continued to sell despite being anything but fine (in 1961 sales of Canadian wine rose 8.6% in the LCBO), and despite being inhibited by the nature of the only grapes available. Experiments with both French hybrids and *vinifera* by wineries like Brights and Parkdale (a Toronto-based winery that had had some success growing Riesling and Gamay in Niagara) had generated some interest in the industry but little change in what was being grown and planted in vineyards. Unfortunately, work at the Horticultural Research Institute continued to be focused more on crop yield than on quality and on developing their own new hybrids that would grow successfully for the farmers. The researchers had an unfortunate aversion to *vinifera* grapes, which were regarded more as a stumbling block than a stepping stone for improving the fortunes of growers. As a result, when the industry was challenged by forces it could not control, it simply found itself unprepared and unable to respond, allowing its reputation once again to be assailed.

Grape growers needed reassurance that the new varieties would grow as well as what they were being asked to replace and, quite naturally, they were slow to buy into immediate or significant change.

When I met them, Bill and Helen Lenko were typical of Ontario growers in the late 1940s and 1950s growing both a variety of fruits and Concord grapes on their 28-acre farm on the western outskirts of Beamsville. In 1960 Bill received 2,000 Chardonnay vines from Parkdale winery; he planted them, although he knew very little about the variety. They survived and soon he was selling Chardonnay grapes to a winery that simply blended them in with their other grapes at that time. Bill was inspired to plant other new vines after tearing out all his Concord grapes in 1975, including a little-known blue French hybrid grape the French called Leon Millot (Kuhlmann 194-2), a sister grape of the more well-known Marechal Foch. This grape made an excellent red wine for myself as an amateur winemaker, as Bill allowed me to hand-pick only the best grapes I could find on his vines. Unfortunately, that grape would not survive, but by then Bill was planting Merlot and Pinot Noir and Gewurztraminer and establishing a well-earned reputation for quality. Thanks to the Lenkos and other growers, who risked their livelihood on untried hybrid and *vinifera* vines and worked unbelievably hard in the process, gradually enough tonnage of these new varieties would become available for the wineries to make new varietal wines. Many of these growers, including Bill Lenko, would go on to become "Grape Kings" in the industry, producing grapes that would allow for the future revitalization of the wine industry, especially Bill's Old Vines Chardonnay, which would produce numerous awards for myself at Stoney Ridge Cellars after 1985.

By the early 1960s the post-war boom in Ontario had resulted in a more affluent society This new generation had more leisure time and disposable income and opted for a more liberal life style. Tastes in wine were beginning to change. People travelled more, learned more about wine, and enjoyed wines that were different from those made in Ontario, for the most part wines that were drier, certainly less alcoholic, and generally more sophisticated. Also changing was the concept of wine's role. No longer did wine merely provide an escape from reality (perhaps in a dark alley). Now it was a pleasurable adjunct to life. It was served with meals and used to entertain friends and was becoming part of everyday life.

This period marked my first real involvement with a beverage that I had seldom enjoyed before, except for the traditional glass or two at Christmas or on other noteworthy occasions. I remember fondly how, at a family dinner to celebrate my graduation from McMaster University in 1964, I opened a bottle of Bright's President Champagne with considerable fanfare, and this was indeed a rare occurrence. After I started my teaching career in 1965 I began to explore wine with more interest like many of my friends and discovered a world of pleasure that I wanted to know more about. We fell in love with Mateus, a fizzy, sweetish rose from Portugal and Castlevetro, as well as a red crackling wine from Italy, and sweeter Germanic offerings including Blue Nun and Liebraumilch. These wines represented my evolution from "pop"—I never did enjoy drinking beer and wondered what all the excitement was about—and tended to be sweet, fruity, and very tasty. Ontario wine was simply left behind, as drinking sherry or port and the other native grape wine concoctions available then held no interest for me, apparently something I shared with many other novice wine drinkers in the mid 1960s.This was the time of the so-called British invasion in music, featuring the Beatles first and foremost, and the "European invasion" in wine. Both would have a game-changing impact on our culture, literally drowning out 'the good old days' and opening the doors to a new future. For many the word 'wine' now meant European wine, more pleasant and appealing overall, with intriguing labels, and not expensive. For those who appreciated such things, you could buy a first-growth Bordeaux at this time for what now seems the unbelievable price of just $5!

Faced with a more discriminating consumer, even the LCBO felt challenged and was convinced to make changes. By 1965 their store system had grown from the original 80 back in 1927 to 362, to provide better service to consumers, and now management was making an effort to improve the appearance of what had been sterile store interiors and creating a more user-friendly atmosphere, all while still controlling the orderly sale of alcoholic beverages. The need for customers to produce a sales permit and to sign for purchases disappeared and some stores began as early as 1963 to display Ontario wines behind glass for consumers to see before purchase (but not touch!). Changes later in the 60's would see Ontario's first self-service store and the arrival in Toronto of the first "Rare Wine" store, the precursor of today's Vintages channel. In the LCBO, individual listings of Ontario wines approached 200, about one-half the number of imported brands which continued to increase with the sales of foreign wines, confirming the evolving trend for different and finer wine. The proof was in the pudding, for by 1968 the once non-existent table wine category had risen to 32% of the overall wine market!

Ever so slowly, the industry was beginning to recognize the necessity of improving wine quality with increased plantings of the newer varieties, while at the same time maintaining market share with the old. The year 1964-5 saw the introduction of a new category of wines. They became an overnight craze—inexpensive wines doctored with flavours like juniper and with catchy names like Zing and Riki and Sangria. Sales soared for two years and overall wine production increased to 6,720,000 gallons.

By 1966 French hybrids had reached 10% of vineyard plantings with Chelois (S 10878) accounting for over half of this, followed by Marechal Foch (Kuhlmann 188-2) at 2%, and the white S 9110 (named Verdelet in 1970) at only .3%. Seibel 9549, which had reached 99 tons in 1963, was at 1.4%, but it would soon become the overall preferred variety when some of the other hybrids began to have growing pains. Some of the first planted hybrids like Verdelet, Aurora, and Chelois, were failing in the vineyard, leaving growers to question the viability of such vines. The *labrusca* varieties still dominated at 85%, 50% red and 35% white, with Concord leading all varieties at 43% of harvest. There are no statistics for *vinifera* varieties at this time, but wineries continued to experiment with the small crop available. This same year marked the retirement of Adhemar De Chaunac, whose work at Bright's Wines and with many others in the Ontario grape and wine industry serve as the first chapter in our revised new winemaking history. His contributions to the future were formally acknowledged in 1972 after his death when the Ontario wine growers renamed the blue grape Seibel 9549 in his honour, a fitting tribute for the man who had introduced French hybrids to the province.

As several writers have commented, the dawn of a new decade in 1970 would prove to be the watershed for the Ontario Grape and Wine Industry, the line separating the flow of Concord of the past from the future river of world-class wine. Not one incident or event, and not one single person created this line, but after ten years of change in every aspect of the business, it was clear our wine industry had moved in a different direction. And no one was anxious to turn back.

The decade began with the sale of a winery located in Winona named Beau Chatel, and owned by Imperial Tobacco. Its origins dated back to Prohibition as Subosits Wines (later becoming Welland Wines and moving to Winona), but the sale did not represent a further consolidation of the industry. The winery was purchased by a fascinating Hamilton entrepreneur named Andrew Peller, who had been a grocer, as well as an owner of a car dealership, an ice company, a brewery, and newspaper. In 1961 he moved to B.C. from Hamilton and opened a very successful winery in Port Moody. The winery in Winona, located prominently along the south service road by the Queen Elizabeth highway, represented new blood in the Ontario wine industry and, before long, the appropriately named Andres Wines would be a household word.

The 1971 harvest produced a huge crop of 84,000 tons of grapes and the industry was drowning in Concord. Inspired by a novelty wine in the United States named Cold Duck, which was made from the Concord, Peller created a blend of Concord (70%) and Niagara (30%) which he called Baby Duck. Baby Duck was an easy-drinking, fruity, sweet, carbonated concoction with only 7% alcohol, an inexpensive wine that Peller dressed up with gold embossing and foil, with rich purple labels showing a cute, tiny, yellow duckling. The wine became an overnight marketing success, the largest-selling wine in the province. Soon it accounted for one out of every 24 bottles of wine sold in Canada. And for the two years between 1977-1978, Baby Duck was the top selling wine in Canada, a feat that no other Canadian wine has achieved since!

The wine opened with a pop. And it tasted like pop. Other wineries swiftly followed suit. Soon consumers could choose from a whole zoo full of what consumers called 'pop' wines. These pop wines bore names like Baby Bear, Baby Deer, Pink Flamingo, Gimli Goose, Sno-bird, Pussycat, and Fuddle Duck. A zoo indeed! The industry dubbed this category "refreshment wines" as they could be enjoyed on any occasion, not just with a meal, and they certainly refreshed the bank accounts of both wineries and growers throughout the 70's. Andrew Peller commented that "Canadian wine-making has come of age," but the wines that were indeed a godsend and huge business success were actually considered by wine lovers to be not worthy of the name "wine." Derision and snorts of laughter were elicited at the mere mention of the name Baby Duck and no real wine drinker would ever admit to trying these fizzy and fun creations. Ironically, although these pop wines had literally saved the Ontario grape and wine industry at a time when other high volume products such as the traditional ports and sherries were losing popularity, they achieved nothing in changing its unfortunate reputation.

Sad to say, given how the industry otherwise over-looked or ignored the taste preferences of consumers, it became the norm to criticize the quality of Ontario wine. Any comparison with imported wines involved a lack of respect for our native wines that had no bounds. Heading the list of those who avoided our wines was the Federal Government that insisted on serving imported wines and not Canadian at official functions out of fear of losing "all our friends." Several prominent people took the opportunity to ridicule the industry, including noted author Mordecai Richler who proclaimed: "There is only so much plonk I am able to drink for my country!" And actor Christopher Plummer in 1974 declared, as if on stage, "Canadian wines? My God, they're terrible! I had a glass on the train from Montreal, and my hand nearly fell off." Two years earlier, famed English wine expert Hugh Johnson, when asked his opinion of our wines, answered bluntly: "The foulness of taste is what I remember best—an artificially scented, soapy flavor." Comedian and satirist Henry Gibson was just as cruel proclaiming, "Ontario wines? Hah! I wouldn't even wash my car with them." Restaurants were reluctant to serve Ontario wines, aside from the occasional bottle of Bright's President Champagne or Baby Duck, and there was virtually no media commentary or promotion of them. No wonder that many consumers, who were now keen on drinking wine, believed that if it was a local wine it probably was not worth drinking, and if it was imported it must be good.

With my own awakening interest in wine drinking at this time came a desire to learn more about wine in general, including its history and how wine was made, subjects about which I knew very little. By 1970 I was increasingly buying imported wines for what I tried to justify as research, purchasing three or four wines at a time from a specific region in France or Italy or somewhere else in the wine world and reading about those particular wines. In the fall I went to a party at the home of my school principal for our new teachers where he allowed me to sample, right from a large glass carboy, some wine he was making. At the time this struck me as being fun and educational and I was inspired to give winemaking a try. I bought some Concord and Niagara grape juices from a farmer in Fruitland who had advertised them in *the Hamilton Spectator*, knowing absolutely nothing about the marvel of fermentation. Little did I know then what this innocent venture would lead to over the coming years for both myself and my family.

Whether it was the quality of the juice itself or my complete lack of winemaking expertise, both the red and white wines I made were undrinkable: thin, sour, and totally unpleasant, so typical of a *labrusca* grape, wine made dry and without any knowledge of wine chemistry. So much for making wine from native grapes! My wife Charlotte still believed that I needed a hobby, and that there was a better way for me to make wine. For Christmas she gave me two winemaking kits, which she purchased from a shop called Wine Art, along with a red wine and a peach wine concentrate that would allow me to make wine as easy as baking a cake. The Arthur's family in Toronto had started a small chain of these hobby winemaking shops selling cans of various grape and fruit concentrates and every winemaking supply, likely in response to a growing demand from people interested in making wine and beer at home and expanding their knowledge of the subject, and wanting to do at very modest cost and with none of the work or mess of crushing grapes. Unfortunately, the results again were disappointing, totally lacking in fruitiness and character and somewhat oxidized. It seemed to me that something was being lost in the concentrating process, producing a beverage that resulted in wine in name only. To this day, the remaining bottles of this experience sit in my wine cellar as cloudy testaments to my vinification ignorance of long ago.

I was about to forsake my winemaking dream, along with my glass carboys, when Charlotte asked me one Sunday afternoon to clean out the freezer. I found some older strawberries and red currants and, rather than throwing them away, decided to ferment the lot using up the ingredients I still had available. To everyone's surprise, the rose wine that resulted was delightful, not only good but great compared to my previous efforts. I thought that if I could make such a wonderful thing without knowing what I was doing, how much better wine could I make if I did know more about fermenting.

In Hamilton, the Wine Art store was owned by two interesting characters named Rudi and Verne who appeared to be very knowledgeable about the subject; I proudly took a bottle of my rose to them for their evaluation, hoping they would tell me how to learn more. Rudi liked the wine and invited me to join the Hamilton Wine Circle, a local amateur winemaking club, which was going to have their next meeting at his house. Everyone who came to the meeting brought a bottle of their own wine for tasting and I thought this was just wonderful, but it was Rudi's basement that really knocked me out. There were at least 50 carboys of various kinds of wine, all neatly arranged in what was a mini-winery. At that moment, I knew this was the right hobby for me, and I joined the club, a decision that would set me on a path of learning and discovery about wine that 15 years later would lead to the opening of our winery: Stoney Ridge Cellars, in Vinemount on the farm of my partners Bryce and Jennifer Weylie.

As it turned out, the Hamilton Wine Circle was one of over 40 winemaking clubs located all over the province that belonged to an organization called Amateur Winemakers of Ontario (A.W.O.). In the early 1970's hundreds of members met regularly to discuss and sample both homemade and professional wines and to compete in annual competitions with their wines. At that time no one realized that A.W.O. would become an important player in the renewing of our wine industry and a driving force in spreading the word about the potential of our new grapes for making wines that was every bit as good as those made by the wineries. A.W.O. built a relationship with many of the up-and-coming new winemakers and with grape growers, while seeming to fly under the radar because of its amateur status, a term which usually implies something less than professional. But many of the members were extremely passionate about their hobby as true 'wine lovers' and dedicated themselves to making very high-quality wines. In the years to follow, A.W.O. became a source of several well-respected Ontario winemakers, as a number of individuals who started winemaking as members of an A.W.O. club would go on to a careers in the wine industry. The risk in naming these individuals is that I will overlook someone, but as of this time I believe that all of these winemakers came from the ranks of A.W.O.: Don Ziraldo of Inniskillin, Joe Pohorly of Newark Wines and Joseph's Estate Wines, Frank Zeritsch of 30 Bench Winery, the late John Marynissen of Marynissen Estates, Eddie Gurinskas of Lakeview Cellars, Ron Sperazini of Willow Heights (Green Lane), Terry Rayner of Coffin Ridge, John Tummon of Kacaba Winery, and myself. It is difficult to imagine the Ontario wine industry without the contributions of such people!

Despite changes taking place in the wine business, since Ontario wine sales were still significant, the wineries continued to believe that the *labrusca* varieties had a meaningful role to play in the industry. Between 1973 and 1977, Ontario sales increased from 5,496,836 gallons to 6,244,954 (13.6%), while imported sales soared from 3,323,188 gallons to 6,056,888 (82%). But when there was a formidable surplus of grapes in 1976, the industry decided to pressure the Ontario government for help in dealing with inventory issues. The government responded with the Ontario Wine Industry Assistance Program, an attempt to promote Ontario wines in LCBO stores by providing the stores with more shelf space. They also delisted poor-selling imported brands and returned more of the selling price of Ontario wine to the wineries. The result would be a pleasant increase of 10 percent in Ontario sales and primarily in the table wine category. At the same time, grape growers received interest-free loans for five years to encourage them to remove old varieties and replant with the new preferred French hybrid and *vinifera* vines.

Such support for both segments of the business represented no change in government policy but maintained an ongoing commitment to assure the viability of a long-standing and important industry in Ontario. However, other government action, as a result of poor grape harvests in 1972 and 1975, with a similar intent, was a step in a completely new direction. To assist wineries faced with a shortage of grapes in 1972, the government urged the Ontario Grape Growers' Marketing Board (OGGMB) to agree to the importation of up to 18,000 tons of grape concentrate to make up 80% of the shortfall, as long as the wineries made no new blends with the product. Prior to this, with the exception of four years during Prohibition when US grapes were allowed in (1926-1930), Ontario wine was always made from grapes grown exclusively in the province. This policy had always assured the growers that the wineries would annually be obligated to buy up the entire crop, even though the relationship between buyer and seller when it came to establishing prices was not always the best. Now, many were pushing for importation, initiating an argument over the meaning of Canadian wine that continues to this day.

A more dramatic development followed in 1976 when the government changed the Wine Content Act to allow wineries, for a five-year period, to import grapes or wine for blending purposes. This would compensate for the shortage of grapes and provide the potential to improve wine quality. Not everyone was happy with the change in regulations. Ontario grape growers felt threatened, fearing that in the future the wineries might no longer want to buy local grapes, but the wineries were restricted to importing only up to 15% of their production and to using a maximum of 30% in any one wine blend with a new limit of 225 gallons of wine from a ton of grapes established (down from 250) as an appropriate concession. Wineries reassured growers that all of their grapes would continue to be required and that new branch plants were being built across Canada and new wines were forthcoming.

Some might have been concerned that no longer would Ontario Wine necessarily contain 100% local material. The wineries, however, believed that blending would improve the taste profile of their table wines and used imported *vinifera* material to enhance the available hybrids, both American and French. As controversial an issue as it was, blending brought immediate positive changes to the mix of Ontario wines, giving wineries the ability to be more competitive by creating new and more desirable wines and by broadening their portfolios. Unfortunately, the controversy has never gone away, becoming a conundrum for a wine industry today where the so-named "Blended in Canada" wines produced by the larger wineries far outsell 100% Ontario VQA wines and serve only to divide an industry where less than 5% of all wineries enjoy the privilege of producing blended wines.

With all the noise surrounding the changes in regulations it would be easy to overlook what was happening in Ontario vineyards, where things mattered most. By 1972 the French hybrids that had originally arrived in Ontario with only a producer's name and number had at last received official names, and growers had been convinced to plant a wide selection of these varieties as well as several different *vinifera*. Some of the grapes either did not grow well or did not make acceptable wine, but others were proving successful and soon white hybrids like Seyval Blanc and Vidal and numerous other reds including Villard Noir, Chambourcin, Foch, Baco, and De Chaunac would be producing sufficient tonnage for winemaking. Seibel 9549 was renamed "De Chaunac" in honour of Bright's retired winemaker Adhemar de Chaunac , for his role in bringing French hybrids to Ontario—the first and only hybrid to be named for an Ontario winemaker! De Chaunac was by far the most heavily-planted new variety with almost 6300 tons harvested in 1977, a year that will be remembered in our wine history as being the first time in our winemaking history that the so-called "preferred varieties" of new hybrids and *viniferas* produced more tonnage than the traditional *labrusca* varieties. And already the de Chaunac grape was being labeled "the new Concord" by many in the industry, with some wineries using it to produce sherry and attempting to use it even for the making of white wine in addition to red wine.

That year Concord was still responsible for almost 25% of the vintage, but new grapes, including *viniferas* like Gamay, Riesling, and Chardonnay along with the French hybrids represented 54% of the total harvest. Brights was moving ahead with experimental plantings in Essex and Kent Counties and interest was awakening in planting vines on Pelee Island once again. Other changes would be in store for Ontario's vineyards as growers became aware of the need to produce better quality grapes, of the need for more expertise in using new technologies to achieve this, and of the need to plant a wider selection of *vinifera* grapes despite the challenges involved. Who could deny at this time that the future of the industry was looking very bright indeed?

By 1977 success in growing the new grapes had already been instrumental in inspiring the LCBO to re-think their policy on the granting of new grape winery licences, something which had not happened in Ontario since the end of Prohibition. A few years earlier the LCBO had been approached by a grower and nursery owner named Don Ziraldo and his partner, a winemaking friend named Karl Kaiser, about the possibility of starting a winery in Niagara-on-the-Lake. They managed to convince the Chairman of the LCBO, General George Kitching, to allow them to make a small amount of wine for what would be a pilot project. Two licences would be necessary, one to make wine for LCBO approval, and a second to allow the sale and listing of the wine by the LCBO. Inniskillin's first effort, a De Chaunac Rose, was approved by the LCBO and the winery received its sales licence in 1975, becoming the first new grape winery in Ontario in over 40 years.

The initial three wines produced by Inniskillin were made exclusively from four French hybrid red grapes from the 1974 harvest: De Chaunac, Chelois, Foch, and Chancellor. Consumers rushed to buy the limited amounts available upon release. The wines were dry, European in style, and of a quality sophisticated enough to impress! The LCBO trial was deemed an immediate success, and Ontario had a new breed of winery, labeled "cottage" or "boutique." These labels were primarily given because Inniskillin's size meant it was only able to make a few thousand gallons, and also because the Inniskillin winery was artisanal and rustic in appearance—quite different from the other factory-sized existing wineries.

The Hamilton Wine Circle was fortunate to arrange a visit to Inniskillin at this time for a tour and a tasting in a large Quonset hut that had been converted into a make-shift winery where Karl Kaiser was crafting his new wines. One wine we tasted that night was made from a French hybrid grape called Couderc Muscat, a white grape that none of us had ever heard of before, that made a highly aromatic wine with an appealing flavour. I immediately made up my mind to find some of these grapes for my own winemaking. As luck would have it, I met Jake and Helga Froese, who were growers in Niagara; they were willing to sell me a few bushels of Couderc from their extensive planting. Those grapes made three wines: a table wine, a sparkling wine, and a dessert wine, all of which I entered in the A.W.O. annual competition, winning three gold medals and becoming the Ontario Champion Amateur Winemaker! Later that year the same wines would win me the Canadian Championship. My first award as a commercial winemaker would come a few years later in 1986 when a wine made from Couderc

Muscat won a bronze medal for Stoney Ridge Cellars in an International Competition, setting us on a path to become one of Ontario's most awarded wineries. To Karl I owe a debt of gratitude for introducing me to the grape that would inspire me to make wine at a more serious level, an inspiration that would eventually become my second career.

In September 1973, a second "pilot" was approved by the LCBO, providing a group of Niagara businessmen headed by Karl Podamer—a Hungarian with a sparkling winemaking background—an experimental licence to produce sparkling wine and champagne in a sprawling building on Ontario Street in Beamsville. Karl planned to use French hybrid grapes to make high-quality wine in brand-new 500-gallon casks of Austrian white oak that were assembled in the winery by barrel makers from Austria. The wine would then be bottled for its secondary fermentation in some 120,000 bottles for the first vintage, which would then be aged in their extensive ground-level cellars. The Podamer Champagne Co. Ltd., received their winery licence and ability to sell their wines just a few days after Inniskillin, and would have their "fermented in the bottle" sparkling wines on sale at their official opening in September, 1975.

The wines from these two wineries were a revelation to both wine critics and the industry and offered proof that Ontario was finally capable of producing wine that could be appreciated world-wide. Although the initial production was small and out-of-proportion to the reputation it inspired, the wines made a significant impact on consumers and paved the way for wave after wave of other small wineries that would eventually change the image and identity of the Ontario wine industry.

Before the end of the decade, three additional new wineries would open, all small family businesses as opposed to corporate entities, businesses that were serious about their intentions to elevate the quality of Ontario winemaking. Charlotte and Allan Eastman, who had some 30 varieties of hybrids and *vinifera* grapes planted near Blenheim in Kent County, initiated a revival of winemaking in southwestern Ontario, making their first experimental wine in 1975. The mere 1,000 gallons of white wine included a Chardonnay that won a gold medal in its first competition two years later, the same year their winery licence was approved as Charal Winery and Vineyards. To differentiate themselves from other wineries, their intention was to produce only varietal wines from their own grapes and therefore all identified as "Estate Bottled."

At the same time the Bosc family—Paul, his wife Andree, and their two sons Paul and Andre—started their winery, Chateau des Charms, near St. David's, amidst 58 acres of *vinifera* vines planted in 1978. Paul Bosc had emigrated from Algeria in 1963, eventually becoming the winemaker at Chateau-Gai before opening his own winery. Paul believed strongly that *vinifera* grapes could be grown successfully in Niagara and make world-class wines. He quickly became a leader in their production, developing a loyal following for the quality of the results. Their first winery was a rather simple stone building on Creek Road that belied the quality of the wines inside. When I visited in late 1979, I recall being struck by the elegance of the wines we tasted. In that small sampling room managed by Andree, I could sense that this winery would have a huge impact on the wine industry. Indeed, the initial wines made from French hybrid and *vinifera* grapes brought them immediate acclaim; before long, the family opened an impressive "Chateau" on Highway 8 on the St. David's Bench that has become a mecca for wine lovers world-wide.

One year later Joe and Betty Pohorly opened Newark Winery on their fruit farm in Niagara-on-the-Lake, the fifth new boutique-sized winery in Ontario in just five years. Joe was a teacher and self-taught winemaker who saw the market that was developing for wines made from the French hybrids and *vinifera* grapes, the same grapes that he was growing. In 1979, his first vintage, he managed to produce just over 5,000 gallons, including a Gewurztraminer—a spicy, fragrant *vinifera* wine that was still very rare in Ontario. With his wife and two daughters helping to make and sell the wines, Joe's "Newark" brand became an overnight success and attracted the attention of a German corporation, Hillebrand, which a few years later would purchase the winery. This was the first of several foreign buyers that would become attracted to the Ontario Wine Industry down the road.

These new wineries symbolized everything that the established industry had been unable to achieve in 100 years of winemaking: the production of quality driven, innovative dry table wines made from grapes other than the *labrusca*, wines that could earn consumer respect. Thus, the arrival of these boutique wineries in the province could be considered either the culmination of a wine revolution (initiated by Brights and Adhemar de

Chaunac in the 1930s) or a renaissance of winemaking led by new wine makers who were prepared to leave the past behind. Along with growers who risked their future on the new grapes, these winery proprietors showed considerable courage and daring in attempting to become winemakers at a time when the wine industry was under attack and failing. They should be commended for what they did, why they did it, and how, through sacrifice and hope, they managed to achieve success.

By the end of the decade, Ontario consumers enjoyed an incredible and unprecedented choice of wines available at a growing number of LCBO stores and at wineries where, since 1977, they could now take cellar tours, enjoy sample tastings, and purchase wines. Although imports were now outselling Canadian wines, and older wineries continued to add to their listings of refreshment wines, ports, and sherries (10 new sherries appeared in Ontario alone in 1977), the wine industry now had a chance to compete with the popular, top-selling imported brands on price, quality, and variety. Virtually every winery was offering new and exciting blends of imported material with *labrusca* and/or French hybrid grapes that were labeled with European sounding names to capitalize on the "foreign is better" beliefs of the buyer—think of Domaine D'Or, Grande Cuvee, Botticelli, Maria Christina, Toscano, Rhinekeller, Hochtaler, and countless more. Often these wines were presented as "light table wines" to appeal to those wanting less alcohol. And both established wineries and the new boutique wineries were impressing consumers with an extensive range of single grape varietals that few wine drinkers had heard of before 1970, including French hybrids like De Chaunac, Villard Noir, Chambourcin, Foch, Verdelet, and Seyval Blanc and Viniferas including Riesling, Chardonnay, Gamay, and Gewürztraminer. The arrival almost overnight in the mid 1970's of a plethora of new and unfamiliar wine names was at first somewhat confusing for the average consumer, but it signaled a change in the industry that would not be reversed, serving as a prelude for many more new grapes and wine to follow.

Although it might have seemed strange in 1976 to see two new Ontario wines promoted during the Canada Cup Ice Hockey Event (versus Russia), many wine drinkers were enticed to try what was for them a new taste in Ontario wine—Rubi Red and Golden Castle. They found both to their liking. But it was one wine launched by Chateau-Gai in 1978 that best summed up the decade's achievements of the wine industry. Alpenweiss—a blend of California grapes and Ontario Seyval Blanc, packaged and labeled to provide a European look and feel—was promoted with the slogan "We can change your mind!" When it beat the top-selling German Black Tower in a tasting one year later, the industry truly believed that it was well on its way to changing minds.

And so it was. No longer did our wine industry have to accept the comic derision heaped on our wines or offer excuses for our winemaking!

CONCLUSION

Throwing the baby out with the bathwater, radically!

Why do they even bother to grow grapes to make fine wine in Ontario? The climate is marginal. The places where premium grapes do grow are small, and the memory of an old industry with abysmal quality lingers.

—Bramble, *Niagara's Wine Visionaries*, 2009

The small players had become the engine that propelled Ontario wines, dragging the large commercial players reluctantly along in their combined wake.

—Aspler, *Canadian Wineries*, 2013.

Long ago, some 150 years now, a small number of individuals dared to open wineries across the province, confronting numerous challenges that, from the outset, put the success of their ventures at considerable risk. The raw material they used was a mix of North American *labrusca/vinifera* hybrids, some created spontaneously in nature, others hybridized by man. Although they had to bear the stigma of being "foxy," these were the only vines able to survive in our cold-climate. Despite their unique character that precluded labeling them as "fine wine," the wines they made sold locally, across Canada, and to an international market and were not out-of-step with their time, even claiming awards in several competitions and enabling a grape and wine industry to gain a foothold in Ontario.

Unfortunately, this part of our wine history and the achievements of the industry's founding fathers are not well-known or appreciated today, and the role of the early wine industry along with its North American hybrid grapes as the foundation for our current world-class grape and wine industry and wine culture is considered to be redundant. The years following World War I and up to World War II are still remembered but usually for the wrong reason, given the abysmal quality of much of the wine that was made during Prohibition, and given the clean-up and downsizing afterwards.

Other varieties of grapes were brought to North America after the Second World War. These newer hybrids, created in France, which came with a small number of *vinifera*, initiated radical changes in Ontario winemaking—a revolution on a drastic scale but with no bloodshed! After growers finally became experienced in growing *vinifera* grapes successfully in our soils, Ontario vineyards took on a new look that reflected the new vines and the technological advances in viticulture. As well, new wineries were finally allowed to develop and regulations were revised, all serious reforms that marked the beginning of our fine wine future and the end for Ontario's *labrusca*-centric approach to winemaking.

In 1988 the government outlawed the use of North American hybrids like Concord in the making of table wine. As well, most of the numerous French hybrid varieties still growing at that time (including some extensive plantings of grapes like De Chaunac that had already fallen out of favour) were pulled from vineyards with growers encouraged by yet another government support program to replant with the so-called preferred varieties. Not many in the evolving *vinifera*-driven new industry were sad to see them go, viewing them as an obstacle that needed to be removed from the path of our VQA future. And already by this time we were beginning to forget our winemaking past with its once popular high- alcohol sweet ports and sherries, in favour of more elegant red, white, and rose dry table wines. Vanished as well was the unfortunate scorn and ridicule that accompanied our original wine industry, that had now evolved into a true world-class grape and wine industry.

Throwing the baby out with the bathwater, radically!

Through the 1980's the developing industry witnessed the arrival of one new small winery after another, all anxious to be involved in changing the reputation of Ontario wine. In just a few years consumers would be excited to sample from Colio, Vineland Estates, Reif, Stoney Ridge, Konzlemann, Cave Springs, Henry of Pelham, and many others who were making their contributions to the 'new' industry. Beginning with the closing of Turner Wines in 1977, many of the long-established wineries, now losing market share, became caught up in a second wave of consolidation. Jordan Wines was purchased by Brights in 1986 and Barnes was sold to Chateau-Gai two years later. Chateau-Gai changed their name to Cartier in 1989 and two years later joined with Inniskillin. This was followed by a merger with Brights, who then bought London Wines. In short order the wine industry lost five of its old-guard, but was well on its way to an exciting future with an ever-increasing number of new wineries making award-winning wine from some 20 different *vinifera* varieties.

The loss of our original grapes, historical wines and older wineries was the price the industry paid for its survival, obligating it to throw out the baby with the bathwater. Yet the role these original grapes played in the birth and development of winemaking in Ontario was significant. Without them, we would never have had a grape and wine industry, and all the resulting economic activity that it produced province-wide over a tremendously important century in our history.

The development of Ontario's first or native wine industry has been a fertile field of interest for myself for many years, eventually blossoming into a course at Niagara College which I taught in their Winery and Viticulture Technician Program. It provides abundant material for a good story with many fascinating personalities confronting constant challenges and a continual flow of antagonists from the Temperance movement and Prohibition, the Depression, two World Wars, to foxy grapes themselves. Through all the conflict, the industry proved itself to be a survivor until confronted by dissatisfied and critical consumers who became enamoured of imported wines. Fortunately, the story has a happy ending, inspired ironically by a tiny, destructive bug called *Phylloxera vastatrix*, that led to the transition from Concord grapes to Cabernet and Chardonnay.

Our revolutionized industry already has its own story to tell, complete with its own new challenges from brutal winters to ladybugs to the explosive growth of new wineries. It could make for a provocative sequel!

The end of the beginning: A post mortem for the King!

> In purely commercial terms, the introduction of the Concord grape in the early 1850's was perhaps the single most important development in Eastern viticulture in the nineteenth century. Within a few years the Concord grape was to account for approximately 75% of the grape acreage in the East and, it has been estimated, 90% of its profits.
>
> —Cattell, *The Wines of the East,* 1980.
>
> A decade later (1930-31) consumption was 2,208,807 gallons – for Ontario alone! And 80% of it was a red port-style wine of maximum alcoholic strength made from the Concord grape.
>
> — Aspler, *Vintage Canada,* 1983.
>
> In the same year as the Free Trade Agreement (1988), the Wine Content Act in Ontario was revised and '*labrusca*' varieties were banned from table wines.
>
> —*The World of Niagara Wine* ,2014.

Our journey from the discovery of wild grapes in Eastern North America to the demise of their foxy successors in Ontario some four centuries later has come to an end.

Looking back, we can trace this journey from its beginning in early 17th century America to its destination—the successful growing in Ontario of *vinifera* grapes, a species that is not indigenous to North America—following a route that was by no means direct and certainly not pre-planned. Those who take the outcome today for granted may wish to believe it was pre-destined, but that is hardly the case. Indeed, we have seen that it was first sheer good luck along with much human suffering and then human

Throwing the baby out with the bathwater, radically!

ingenuity and no destiny which have resulted in the production of our world-class wines.

If the importation of *vinifera* grapes to the British colonies had resulted in success (or even if the wild grapes had made good wine!) then the course of winemaking in eastern North America would have been much different. But America proved a hostile environment to the *vinifera's* health, frustrating all who made the effort to grow them over the next three centuries. Yet, the very presence of *vinifera* vines among other species here allowed a natural, spontaneous hybridization to occur, with the *labrusca* species in particular, that resulted in the chance creation of new and unique vines displaying characteristics of both parents. This random happening produced the first recorded inter-specific American hybrid, the Alexander, discovered by chance in the 1740's by a gardener who was able to propagate his discovery. For the future of viticulture this was indeed a very lucky happening. More good fortune was to follow. Two other chance hybrids came to light half a century later, the Isabella and the Catawba, inspiring horticulturalists to make significant plantings of these vines in the early 19th century.

With these grapes, it was possible at last for early enthusiasts to make acceptable local wine, the drink of moderation long desired by leading citizens like Thomas Jefferson, speaking for many when he made his famous comment that "no nation is drunken when wine is cheap," adding that wine was "in truth the only antidote to the bane of whiskey." Without these hybrids, American wine would have remained the unpalatable stuff from wild grapes, and we may never have had the development of vineyards in eastern North America, including Upper Canada, nor experienced the birth of a native wine industry in the north at all!

At the same time, the discovery of these new grapes set in motion a sequence of other unplanned happenings that had additional fortuitous consequences.

The renewed interest in grapes that these early hybrids inspired soon led to a mania of hybridization as individuals hoped to improve on Mother Nature by developing their own hybrids that might be more resistant to the environment and produce grapes that would be less foxy or make better wine. There were few real successes. But one of these, first appearing around 1850, would become our most widely-planted grape and the most well-known *labrusca* hybrid of them all.

The Concord, which U.P. Hedrick called "a landmark in the development of American grape culture," was able to adapt to almost any growing conditions while producing consistent, large crops of juicy, dark-blue grapes, "a most handsome grape" prized for its "elasticity of constitution" in Hendrick's marvelous words. "Grapey" in the extreme—and the most foxy of the American hybrids—it quickly found favour as an eating grape and for making jams, jellies, grape cobblers and pies. But it was from other roles that it would earn its fame and secure its place in history. Indeed, it is difficult to imagine how different our grape and wine history would have been if just this one grape had never been discovered and presented to the world!

Although it was not highly valued for making dry table wine (provoking the comment that once you tried a taste of Concord wine you would never forget it), without this grape our fledgling native-wine industry might have withered and died. Almost by itself the Concord carried the wine industry in the North East, including Ontario, through the late 1800's by making inexpensive wines that were sweet and high in alcohol, in step with consumer tastes at that time. Due to its popularity, it was exported in good quantities to Montreal and to Winnipeg for home winemaking purposes as well. And a number of hybridists would use Concord as one parent in creating a number of offspring, including a white grape called Niagara that played important roles in both winemaking and the production of white grape juice despite its very strong foxy flavour.

During Prohibition, consumption of Ontario wine made primarily from the Concord grape skyrocketed, aided by government policy that allowed local wine to be the only form of alcohol that could be legally sold in the province. Who can say what would have happened to the wine industry during Prohibition without such good fortune! Looking back, it seems hard to believe that this one grape, which was suitable for almost any other use but wine, could come to dominate our wine industry as it did. Yet, in 1936, almost ten years after Prohibition, Concord still represented nine-tenths of all native grapes grown in North America. In his winemaking textbook of that year, American author Philip Wagner explained why: "It produces so cheaply and abundantly that it makes a dismal joke of all competition. "The real issue for the future wine industry was that the grape, with its distinctive aroma and extreme foxiness, made a joke of our wines.

Throwing the baby out with the bathwater, radically!

A combination of circumstances had, much earlier, played an important part in the development of the Concord grape and helped to reinforce its popularity. In 1864 Louis Pasteur in France had found a way to prevent wine from spoiling with the use of heat. His work intrigued a Wesleyan Methodist minister (also a physician and dentist) named Dr. Thomas Bramwell Welch, whose only interest in wine was preventing its consumption! In 1865 Welch moved to Vineland, New Jersey, a bone-dry community where there were abundant grapes, and began to experiment with Concord grape juice as a substitute for what was called raisin water in his church's communion service. Methodists, opposed to any form of alcohol, were somewhat uncomfortable with the thought of the grape juice actually fermenting. By 1869 Welch had invented a method of pasteurizing the juice to produce a non-alcoholic communion wine from undiluted, unsweetened, and unfermented grape juice that tasted much better than raisin water. Fortunately, both Pasteur and Welch both lived at the right moment in history!

Other churches used Welch's unfermented Concord wine and gradually what had become a sideline to his normal life became a full-fledged business involving his son Charles. In 1893 they officially launched Welch's Grape Juice Company and soon opened a processing plant in Westfield, New York. The rest is (grape juice) history!

A number of temperance activists led by the ladies of the Women's Christian Temperance Union (WCTU) saw in grape juice an opportunity to bring the commercial wine business to its knees as part of their campaign to eliminate the use of alcohol in the province. They encouraged growers to uproot their other wine grapes and plant Concord, "the grape for the millions," as famous newspaper man Horace Greeley put it at the time. As the temperance movement gathered momentum, even government officials would be persuaded to use grape juice for their functions in place of wine.

Thomas, the staunch prohibitionist, died in 1903 at the age of 77 leaving an indelible legacy that is still respected. The temperance movement, transformed into a prohibitionist platform, would also have a legacy to offer, both in the United States and in Canada, but unfortunately leaving only bitter memories. And the ubiquitous Concord grape would grow on to take over some 70% of vineyard plantings, eventually making countless bottles of wine, from One Star Port to Mogan David and Manischewitz, to Cold

Duck and our own Baby Duck and other so-called refreshment wines, and slyly outfoxing the prohibitionists!

And overlooked in any criticism of this grape is the fact that between two and three million Concord vines were planted in California in the early 1970s to produce grape juice for blending with California grapes while in Ontario, according to grape breeder Oliver Bradt, as late as 1977 there were still more Concords being planted than any other grape except the French hybrid De Chaunac grape.

After World War II more significant plantings of several of these hybrids would eventually prepare the way for the grape and wine revolution that is the basis of our modern local wine industry. This revolution was instigated by the successful transition to numerous *vinifera* varieties and the uprooting of the American hybrids whose fate was sealed for future winemaking purposes—dry and elegant table wines—by the very nature of the high-alcohol wines and other concoctions they produced.

Today we are growing the one species that, for the longest time, had proven virtually impossible to grow in eastern North America: *Vitis vinifera*. This dominance is due to a fascinating chain of circumstances beginning long ago with the importation of *vinifera* vines to the British colonies and the linking years later to the importation of American hybrids to Europe and all of the developments that followed. When it comes to considering our present-day ability to grow *vinifera* in Ontario, it is sobering to realize that this might never have happened without the development of remedies for grape diseases that evolved to deal with mildews arriving in Europe, or without the knowledge about grapevines and root selections that *Phylloxera* inspired to the benefit of *vinifera* grape growing world-wide, or without those French hybrids that might never have been created as a possible solution to the disaster. We would never have had the Baco Noir, Foch, Seyval, and Vidal wines that showed so much promise only 40 years ago, opening the door to our vinous future. Without Vidal alone, the grape used to make our first ice wines, would we have been able to establish the reputation we now enjoy for producing world-class wine? And where would we be if we still were unable to grow Chardonnay, Riesling, Pinot Noir, and so many other *vinifera* varieties?

How amazing that it all began with foxy grapes, the very grapes our wine industry has condemned to infamy and no longer tolerates, the first mysterious link in the chain.

Today science has established the nature of "the fox" in the vineyard with discoveries in aroma chemistry that date to the early twentieth century. A compound called methyl anthranilate, an ester of anthranilic acid with a smell reminiscent of Concord grapes, was identified by researchers as the dominant odor in the grape itself. This compound was present, though less prominent, in many other *labrusca* hybrids, often showing up in wine as a strawberry-like character. Indeed, strawberries also contain methyl anthranilate, as do other fruits like lemons, oranges, and apples, and several flowers as well.

In the 1970s the Biochemistry section of the Horticultural Products Laboratory at the Research Institute in Vineland, Ontario, began to develop a method of quantifying the flavor quality of grapes, an analysis of various flavour components. This involved determining the total volatile esters of various grapes as an index of flavour quality. Many esters can be detected by smell alone, for example, methyl anthranilate, which can be detected at the very low concentrations of 1/10 part in a million! Many grapes with a strong *labrusca* character revealed high methyl anthranilate content, grapes like Concord and Niagara. French hybrids like Foch, De Chaunac, and Chelois, which had little if any *labrusca* in their background, showed virtually no methyl anthranilate and the same was true for several *vinifera* varieties. But there was one curious aspect of all the scientific work. It was discovered that methyl anthranilate was NOT present in many other *labrusca* grapes which also smelled foxy, indicating that there had to be more to foxiness than methyl anthranilate!

In the 1980s, while doing research in Japan, Terry Acree—a professor of Food Science at Cornell University—discovered another compound that was involved with the foxy aroma called ortho-aminoacetophenone. He discovered this quite accidently when a fellow scientist was excising the anal sac of a Japanese weasel. The smell of the sac was identified as ortho-aminoacetophenone. It was the same smell as grapey Concord. Researchers in Europe later discovered that European foxes have this in their scent-marking gland.

Thus, after almost 400 years, we can finally understand why those first European immigrants to the New World chose the word foxy to identify the smell and flavour of the local grapes.

Recently, another study by German scientists has identified a gene on the North American grape chromosome that is responsible for foxy flavours. By genetic modification in breeding hybrids, this gene could be silenced to produce a grape that is disease and pest-resistant like American vines yet with the pure and wonderful flavours of European vines, a hybrid built for growth in North America without any foxy character.

Of course, such a grape could never be called Chardonnay or Pinot Noir, but at least it would allow people who wish to grow grapes and make wine in environments that are too challenging for *vinifera* vines the opportunity to do so—without any fox casting its long shadow over their endeavours!

REFERENCE MATERIAL

When Concord Was King!

Adams, Leon D. *The Wines of America.* McGraw-Hill, San Francisco, 1978.

Aspler, Tony. *Vintage Canada.* Prentice-Hall, Scarborough, 1983.

Bramble, Linda. *Niagara's Wine Visionaries.* James Lorimer and Co. Ltd., Toronto, 2009.

Cattell, Hudson and S. Miller, Lee. *The Wines of the East: Native American Grapes.*

and H Photojournalism, Lancaster, PA. 1978

De Courtenay, J.M. *The Culture of the Vine and Emigration.* J. Darveau, Quebec, 1863.

Hedrick, U.P. *The Grapes of New York.* J. Lyon Co., Albany, N.Y. 1908

Heron, Craig. *Booze – A Distilled History.* Between the Lines, Toronto, Canada, 2003.

Hicks, Kathleen A. *Dixie: Orchards to Industry.* Mississauga Library System.

Innis, Mary Q. *Mrs. Simcoe's Diary.* McMillan of Canada, Toronto, 1965.

Jarrell, Richard A. "Justin de Courtenay and the Birth of the Ontario Wine Industry."

Ontario History. 103:1 (Spring 2011), 81-104.

Johnston, Hugh. *Story of Wine.* M. Beazley, London, 1989.

Masson, Georges. *Wine from Ontario Grapes.* G. Masson, Niagara-on-the-Lake, 1979.

Pinney, Thomas. *A History of Wine in America – From the Beginnings to Prohibition*

(Vol. 1), University of California Press, Berkeley, 1989.

Rannie, W. F. *Wines of Ontario: An Industry Comes of Age.* W.F. Rannie, Lincoln, Ontario, 1978.

Ripmeester, M., Mackintosh, Phillip G., and Fullerton, Christopher, editors. *The World of*

Niagara Wine. Wilfred Laurier University Press, 2013.

Rowe, Percy. *The Wines of Canada.* McGraw-Hill Co., Toronto, 1970.

Rowe, Percy. *Red, White, and Rose.* Musson Book Co., Don Mills, Ontario, 1978.

Tiessen, Ron. *The Vine dressers: A History of Grape Farming and Wineries on Pelee*

Island. Pelee Island Heritage Centre, Second Edition, 1997.

Weber, Lee. *A History of the Vineyard and Wine Industry of Essex County.* 1971, erieshore.ca/history

Innumerable internet sites provided by others, who have shown considerable interest in the early days of our Grape and Wine Industry including older journals and newspapers

Early Hybrid Grapes In Eastern North America

Pre-1800 interspecific primary hybrids

By the end of the 18th century a small number of new grapes had seemingly been discovered by chance growing in the wild in different eastern American states. These attracted the interest of individuals who propagated the vines and shared them with others. This is the rather simple beginning of meaningful viticulture here. Created spontaneously from indigenous wild vines and unknown imported *viniferas*, the resulting grapes generated an early wine industry and led eventually to a similar result in what would become Ontario where previously only native wild species had been available.

The ALEXANDER – 1740s

James Alexander, gardener for Thomas Penn, discovered a vine growing near the Schuylkill River outside Philadelphia close to a place where William Penn had planted *vinifera* vines in the 1680's. This was a black, very foxy hybrid of *labrusca* and unknown *vinifera* parents that became the first North American hybrid to be distributed as a commercial variety. It was known as Tasker's grape after the man who cultivated it in Maryland. It was also called the Schuylkill Muscadel, and was sold by nurseryman Pierre Legaux as the Cape grape to enhance its marketability. Plantings of this grape were known into the

1800's especially in Pennsylvania and it is possible some vines made their way to Upper Canada but there is no specific reference to this grape by name here.

The BLAND – mid 1700s

This grape is said to have been found by Colonel Theodorick Bland (1708-1784) in Virginia and cultivated on his plantation. It is thought to have been a cross between a *labrusca* and a white *vinifera*. It produces a grape that is pale reddish-purple in colour with a mildly foxy flavour. Often referred to as the Madeira grape, it is now believed to be one of the parents of the Norton grape, a hybrid that continues to make acceptable wine in the United States.

The ISABELLA – late 18th century, circumstances unknown

There is some agreement that the vine was discovered near Dorchester, South Carolina where French Huguenots introduced *vinifera* in the 1760's. Cultivated before 1800 this black, foxy *vinifera-labrusca* hybrid was named in 1816 by nurseryman William Prince for Mrs. Isabella Gibbs of New York. It was very popular in Upper Canada where the first reference to it occurs in 1827. However, plantings of Isabella declined after mid-century with the arrival of the Concord grape.

The CATAWBA – circa 1800, origin uncertain

One early tradition traces the origin of the vine to a farm in Asheville, North Carolina, that was owned by a William Murray in 1802. In 1807 General Davy planted cuttings on his farm along the Catawba river and, in 1816, when he was a US Senator, he took some vines to Washington. One ended up at an inn in Maryland owned by a Mrs. Scholl. From this, John Adlum took cuttings in 1819. He soon became the primary proponent of the grape, which he originally called Tokay, only to rename it shortly later. This purplish-red variety is considered to be a *labrusca-vinifera* hybrid with a subdued foxy character. Although it was a notorious late-ripener and prone to mildew, it became the most popular native American grape prior to 1850 due to the efforts of Nicholas Longworth of Cincinnati. The grape came to Pelee Island after mid-century where it was developed into an important variety for our early wine industry.

Early 19th century spontaneous hybrids and the first "man-made" hybrids

In 1830 William Prince published his text *A Treatise on the Vine* in which he gave specific directions for hybridizing American species with "foreign" vines. Soon others would use the previously available hybrids crossed with different *vinifera* to create secondary and other more complex vines. Dr. William Valk of Long Island made his cross by fertilizing Black Hamburg with Isabella to create a grape he called Ada. John Fisk Allen of Salem, Massachusetts used Golden Chasselas to fertilize Isabella in 1843-44 to produce Allen's Hybrid. Thus was laid the foundations for a golden age of grape propagation in eastern North America including Ontario, a propagation that would lead to a massive proliferation in the number of varieties growing here, all in an effort to develop the best grapes possible for table use and for winemaking.

The CLINTON - of confused origin, circa 1820

By the 1840's, a reddish-black grape known as the Clinton was beginning to attract attention for its hardiness and juicy, though acidic, fruit. One story has it that a Mr. Langworthy took cuttings from a vine growing in a garden near the Hudson River and introduced it in 1835 as the Clinton. Another story credits a man named Hugh White who planted a seed in his father's garden in 1819, transplanting the vine in 1821 to

Clinton, New York where he was attending school. The grape is thought to be the same as the Worthington, that is said to have originated near Annapolis, Maryland. It is a hybrid of *Vitis riparia* and *Vitis labrusca* with no *vinifera* parentage and has distinct immunity to *Phylloxera*. It made a foxy wine that took a long time to mellow its acidity.

The DELAWARE – possibly found near Frenchtown, New Jersey, circa 1820's

There is some evidence that this grape, originally called the Heath or Powell after individuals who first grew it, resulted from a seedling of an unknown grape in the garden of a Paul Provost of Frenchtown. In 1849, the editor of the Ohio *Delaware Gazette*, Abram Thompson, sent grapes to a number of people. This resulted in naming the grape after the town. The famous hybridist T.V. Munson believed that one of the parent grapes was an old hybrid named Elsinburgh (*Labrusca-aestivalis*) also from New Jersey The other parent was an unknown *vinifera*. The pale-red grape has an interesting personality, rich and spicy, lacking in foxiness with a lovely flavour and very agreeable aroma, all of which made it the standard for high-quality wines in the early years of the Ontario wine industry.

The DIANA – a seedling planted about 1834 in Milton, Massachusetts

This delicate, light-red variety is thought to have originated from a seedling of Catawba that was planted by a Mrs. Diana Crehor of Milton, and then became another hybrid of *labrusca, aestivalis,* and *vinifera* species. Although it ripened two weeks before Catawba, it lacked winter hardiness and was susceptible to fungi. The grape was used extensively by Barnes Winery, who named a wine after it—Diana!

The CONCORD – born in 1843 in Concord, Massachusetts, raised everywhere!

Ephraim W. Bull (1805-1895) could not have appreciated the viticultural fervor he would generate when he planted a wild grape seed in 1843. The *labrusca* vine from which the seed originated had been transplanted from a field where there was at least one other grapevine growing, the Catawba, which led Bull to say that his wild vine had been fertilized by it. The first fruit came in 1849, and the rest of the story is grape history, as it became "the grape for the millions" according to the famed newspaper man Horace Greeley. Spurred on by the temperance movement, the Concord soon dominated vineyard plantings in eastern North America. The Concord was used for juice—particularly the wildly popular Welch's grape juice—as well as in pies, jams, and jellies, and as an eating grape and for ... wine, foiling both the prohibitionists and those who considered it the worst wine-grape possible. Concord also created innumerable offspring, many white in colour, of which the Niagara grape has been undoubtedly the most successful.

The HARTFORD – a chance seedling found shortly before 1849 in Hartford, Conn.

Named the Hartford Prolific in 1862, this dark-black grape was originally as popular as Concord due to its vigorous, prolific vines. The original vine is said to be a chance seedling that fruited in 1849 in the garden of Paphro Steele of West Hartford; it is considered a hybrid of Isabella and a wild *labrusca* and is distinctly foxy.

The AGAWAM – a Roger's hybrid from 1851 in Salem, Massachusetts

One of numerous seedlings that survived a burst of hybridizing energy by Edward Staniford Rogers of Salem. The female parent used by Rogers was a *labrusca-vinifera* hybrid named Carter or Mammoth Globe, which Rogers fertilized with pollen from two *vinifera* vines: Black Hamburg and White Chasselas. The resulting 35 Hamburg derived seedlings and nine Chasselas were sent to various people for testing. Many of the testers considered these grapes to be of excellent quality, if foxy in flavour. Number 15, perhaps the best of all, was named Agawam, the Indian name of a town in Massachusetts. It was a purplish-red Hamburg cross that became the most widely grown of all the Roger's creations, achieving considerable success in Ontario.

The OPORTO – mysteriously, appearing in New York State c. 1860

A grape very similar to the Clinton. Some say that the Oporto was a *vinifera* brought over from Portugal, as its dark juice made a wine with "the flavour and bouquet of old Port." U.P. Hedrick described it as a cross between *riparia* and *labrusca* (like the Clinton) as it was hardy, resistant to *Phylloxera*, and a good bearer. It was well-received by a number of American grape growers after its introduction by E.W. Sylvester of Lyons, New York in about 1860. In the 1860s, it was listed for sale by W.W. Kitchen of Grimsby along with other vines.

The ELVIRA – a seedling planted in 1863 in Missouri

Elvira was developed by Jacob Rommel of Morrison, Missouri who used seedlings from a *riparia-labrusca* hybrid named Taylor that had been pollinated by a white Concord seedling named Martha. The vine became very popular in Missouri for its hardiness and for the quality of its wine—somewhat foxy but very aromatic. It was also highly valued as being resistant to *Phylloxera*. The greenish-white grape proved to be very popular when it came to Ontario. Though Elvira was widely planted, there is little remaining here today.

The DUTCHESS – created by grape breeder A.J. Caywood in 1868

Dutchess was the most important grape created by Andrew Jackson Caywood of Marlboro, New York. He created it from the seed of a white Concord/Montgomery seedling that was pollinated by Delaware and by another Caywood grape, Walter, a grape named after his son. Thus we have a *vinifera, labrusca, bourquinia, aestivalis* hybrid! This pale yellowish-green grape, which took its name from Dutchess County in New York State, shows virtually no foxy character and made very good quality dry wine.

Early Ontario developed hybrids

With the spread in plantings of these early American grapes, commercial winemaking began to develop in several States and in, after 1860, what was soon to become Ontario. As the 1800's wound down, only a very few of the plethora of other man-made hybrids (like the Niagara) would prove useful for winemaking, despite the fact that several grapes were developed in Ontario by local hybridizers who were searching for more hardy, disease resistant, and early ripening varieties. Although their work was considered impressive at the time, in virtually every case the results were not sustainable, and today the following grapes remain merely of historical interest.

Charles Arnold moved to Paris, Ontario from England (born 1818) at the age of 15 and developed his Paris Nurseries in 1853, creating a number of grapes over the following years.

The Autochon, Arnold's #5, was a white grape developed in 1859 from the Clinton grape and pollinated by Golden Chasselas. When it was introduced it was described as "a veritable treasure." Arnold created several other grapes from the Clinton that were fertilized by Black St. Peters, a *vinifera* variety. Both the Canada (#16) and its brother the Brant proved susceptible to mildew, but came to be grown later in French vineyards destroyed by *Phylloxera*. Two other similar grapes named by Arnold, the Cornucopia (#2) and the Othello, rounded off the significant contribution of the man who was esteemed as "Canada's greatest hybridist" for his remarkable talent in creating new fruits, vegetables, and grains, in addition to his grapes.

A second local hybridizer of note was W.H. Read of Port Dalhousie, one of the founders of the Fruit Growers' Association of Upper Canada.

His contributions included Ontario, a large black grape, Silver cluster, and Lincoln, a seedling of Concord crossed with Black Hamburg. He also contributed Jessica, and Chippewa, a black grape that Read found growing on the banks of the Chippewa creek in Niagara in 1858. A later hybrid from about 1880 was called Moyer, named after Allen Moyer of St. Catharines, who introduced it in 1888. This was a cross of Delaware fertilized by Pinot Meunier that became popular due to its lack of foxiness and its early ripening.

Three other hybridizers—Peter Dempsey of Albury in Prince Edward County, William H. Mills and William Haskins, both of Hamilton—also deserve mention. Dempsey's Burnet was a seedling of Hartford Prolific crossed with Black Hamburg. It gave a large black and juicy berry. The Mills grape was produced about 1870 from a seed of Black Hamburg that was fertilized by Creveling (a grape of uncertain origin but with *labrusca* parentage and very much like Isabella). Haskins' grape, Abyssinia, had an intriguing name. However, like the others it failed to catch on as a significant variety.

The number of grapes created or discovered in the late 18th and 19th centuries is simply stunning and a true indication of the passion that humankind has for grapes. With very few exceptions, these varieties have long ago fallen out of favour in eastern North American winemaking. Far more complex French American hybrids and many *vinifera* varieties have taken their place, finally winning the day in a long and challenging battle to establish a world-class wine industry here. They are now almost forgotten in time. However, as precursors to the wonderful grape and wine industry we now enjoy they can never be completely erased from our vinous history.

ABOUT THE AUTHOR

Jim Warren

Jim Warren became an acclaimed amateur winemaker while teaching languages in a Hamilton high school . In 1985 with his wife Charlotte and two friends he co-founded a boutique winery named Stoney Ridge that would go on to become one of Canada's most awarded wineries. In 2000 he joined the faculty of Niagara College and assisted with the development of the Vineyard and Winery Management Program, acting as both instructor and winemaker. In 1997 Jim was selected as Ontario winemaker of the year and ten years later received the Cuvee Award of Excellence for his contribution to the wine industry. As a consultant Jim has assisted with the creation of numerous new wineries in Ontario. With "When Concord was King!" he has fulfilled a desire to outline the history of Ontario's original wine industry.

www.ingramcontent.com/pod-product-compliance
Lightning Source LLC
LaVergne TN
LVHW091550060526
838200LV00036B/780